PORTLAND WORKS

Stainless Steel Cutlery

Anna de Lange

and others

To Darrell

Anna de Lange.

First published in the United Kingdom by Arc Publishing and Print 2020

All text is copyright © Anna de Lange
and Portland Works Little Sheffield, 2020.
Cover photo: www.carlwhitham.com

All rights reserved.
No portion of this book may be reproduced, stored in a retrieval system or transmitted at any time or by any means mechanical, electronic, photocopying, recording or otherwise, without the prior written permission of the author.

The right of Anna de Lange to be identified as the author of this work has been asserted by her in accordance with the Copyright, Designs and Patents Act 1988.

ISBN: 978-1-906722-74-6

All views, comments and photos printed in this book
are those supplied by the author
and should not be attributed to the publisher.

Contents

Chapter	Page
Introduction and plan	1
The stainless steel story	3
Robert Fead Mosley	15
Heyday – a vision of excellence	25
The end of R F Mosley's era	37
R F Mosley & Co after 1921	49
Portland Works – 1968 to 2010	63
Saving Portland Works	71
Tenants of today	83
Looking to the future	95
Sources and acknowledgements	97

Above: Rusnorstain knives in the Portland Works collection
Below: Advert, probably prior to 1935, for R F Mosley's knives

STAINLESS CUTLERY

FIRST MAKERS

OUR "RUSNORSTAIN" brand was the first rustless cutlery to be offered to the public. Our unique experience in the manipulation and treatment of the new steel enables us to give the best obtainable results in cutting and stainless properties, finish, durability and general efficiency.

We have a well-equipped department for the manufacture of silver and E.P. hollow-ware and spoons and forks. Original and artistic designs are features of our goods.

R. F. MOSLEY & Co., Ltd.
Portland Works   -   -   SHEFFIELD
LONDON SHOWROOMS: Bath House, 59 Holborn Viaduct, E.C. 1

[16]

Portland Works

Introduction

Portland Works is one of the few integrated cutlery works in Sheffield still in use for cutlery-making. It is Grade II* listed, as a building of special architectural or historic interest.

It was built around 1880 by Robert Fead Mosley, pronounced *Mozzley* with a short 'o', who was a Sheffield cutler. Thirty-five years later in 1914 Ernest Stuart, his manager, was the first person ever to find out how to work and market Harry Brearley's stainless steel commercially. He had found a way to forge knife-blades from the newly-discovered material. Every time we use a steel blade, and are able simply to wash it after use, we owe a debt of gratitude to both Ernest Stuart and Robert Mosley as well as to Harry Brearley.

When I first became involved in the campaign to save Portland Works in Sheffield, Mosley's works and the home of this revolutionary experimentation, I wondered about the man who had built such an interesting building, and used it as a base for the manufacture of silverware and cutlery as well as for innovation. Every answer I found posed more questions.

So the story has grown, and I start this new version with an account of the story of 'stainless' steel, which began just before the First World War, and then step well back into the 19th century to find out where Robert Mosley came from and about the start of his business.

This is a considerable expansion of the original book, and contains valuable information gathered from a lot of people. Any errors are my own, but the book is a contribution to the small but important corner of the world that is Portland Works.

To find out more about the Works and what happens there now go to <www.portlandworks.co.uk> where you can also find out how to support and save this historic place of international significance.

So we begin – and I hope you find this story as intriguing as I did.

Portland Works – today's plan

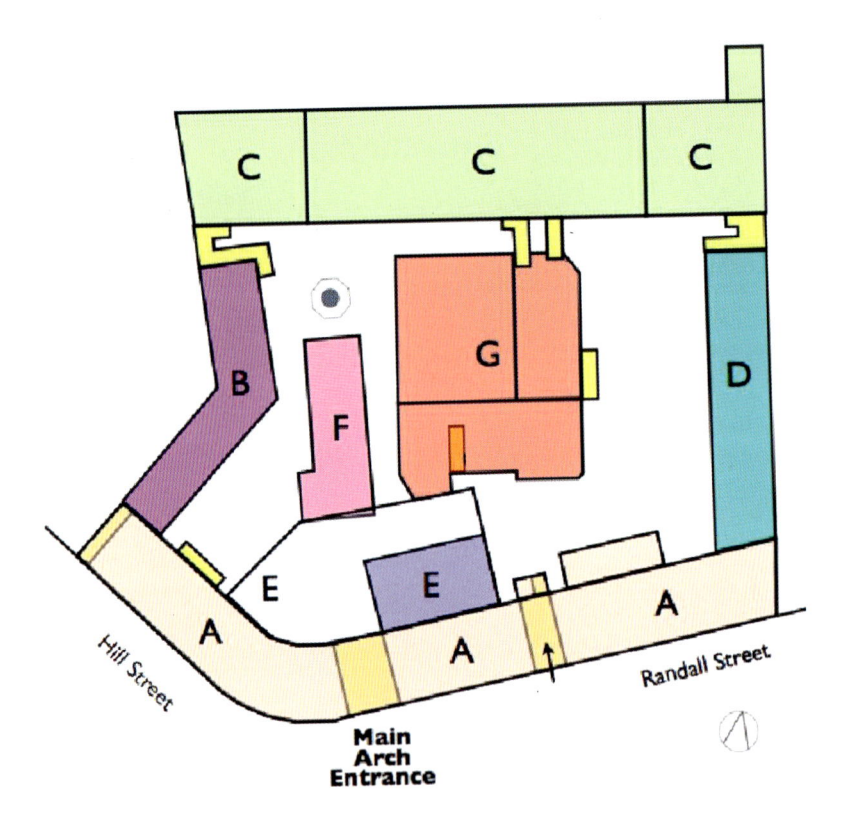

The block numbers on this plan are used from time to time throughout the book – for brevity and for clarity.

The ground-plan today is mostly as it was by 1880, except that block E is around 25 years later, and blocks F and G have been significantly extended from their original form. In broad terms the original functions were placed as follows, giving a circular flow:

- B Hand forging (ground floor)
- C Grinding and buffing
- D Hafting
- E Offices and showroom (later)
- F Engine room, then silver plating
- G Machine forging
- A Inspection and packing

The stainless steel story

Harry Brearley and Ernest Stuart

The rather tangled story of the discovery of stainless steel, and then that the new material can make excellent knife blades, is one of a discoverer, an enterprising business, and an entrepreneurial innovator.[1] In 1914 Ernest Stuart, the R F Mosley cutlery manager at Portland Works, recognised the potential of Harry Brearley's process for making stainless steel. He spent time experimenting, to find a way to manufacture stainless steel knives, after other cutlers had said this could not be done.

Ernest Stuart

We begin with Ernest Stuart, (left) the cutlery manager at R F Mosley's. His was a main drive behind the development of stainless steel other than for munitions. I want to thank the late Pamela Stuart, Ernest's grand-daughter, for the basis of a lot of this story, and also Fiona Lemmon who discussed it with her and recorded what she said.

Ernest's parents and early life

Ernest Stuart was born in 1875 to George and Emily, both of whom seem to have been born in Sheffield. George was a stove and fender grinder. George and Emily had a number of children, but only four survived: Frederick, Ernest, George and Alice. Ernest's grand-daughter said that Robert Fead Mosley was Ernest's godfather, but we do not know how much connection there was between the families at that stage.

Until Ernest married he seems to have lived at home, in the northern (Pitsmoor / Brightside) area of Sheffield. So he could well have attended the same school as Harry Brearley – Brearley discovered that this was one of their connections. However, Brearley was four years older and left school early so they are unlikely to have known each other well.

In 1891 Ernest was a warehouse clerk, but by 1901 he was a table cutlery manager. He married Annie Maria Beesley a little later that year.

By 1911 they were living at 15 Goddard Hill Road, in a house with 7 rooms. Goddard Hill Road still exists, running parallel to Herries Road near the Northern General Hospital. Ernest was 35 and a cutlery manager, his wife Annie 34, and their son Cyril Frederick 9.

We do not know when Ernest began to work for Mosley's. However, by 1914 he was a trusted cutlery manager so had probably been there for several years, and maybe even since 1901. He stayed there for the rest of his life. After 1911 he certainly moved to Ecclesall Road, to be nearer to his workplace at Portland Works.

Rustless steel and Portland Works

Brearley said that 'In June, or possibly July, 1914 I met a cutlery manager who realised that a rustless steel which might be made into table blades would be worth bothering about. I was introduced to Mr. Ernest Stuart by my brother-in-law and found that we had been to school under the same master. Mr. Stuart was sceptical that a rustless steel could possibly exist, but was willing to work the small sample provided into cheese knives, and refused to be helped by any information I could give him about forging temperatures.

'A week later Mr. Stuart produced the knives he had made and pronounced them to be both rustless and stainless; and at that moment, no doubt, his firm's mark 'Rusnorstain' was in his mind. But the steel, said Mr. Stuart, was very hard, and all his adjectival stamping tools [sic!] were ruined. The first knives thus made are still in use, and looking like new in my house.

'Mr. Stuart tried a second time, still refusing help, and produced finished blades without damaging the forging and stamping tools – but such knives! They were brittle and very hard, and when fractured were like cast iron. The steel had been made hot, said Mr. Stuart, so that it would work easily, and he was right about it having been made hot.'

So a third attempt was made, with Brearley in attendance, using 1cwt (about 50kg) of steel bought by Brearley's Amalgams Company from Firth's. Brearley was at pains to point out that the steel was honestly and properly traded, and that Firth's paid for none of the experimental costs. Part of the batch was made into knives and given to friends and family to try out.

There follows an account (found in more than one place, but I have traced this back to source) telling how Ernest Stuart buried one of these first blades in a flowerbed in his garden and left it for three weeks before he dug it up. A 'normal' blade should have rusted badly in that time.

Tested in Flower Pot

Mr C. Stuart, son of the late Mr E. Stuart, who is also with Mosley and Co, told a Sheffield Telegraph reporter yesterday how his father tested the first stainless knives.

'He buried one of them underneath a chrysanthemum plant in our garden,' said Mr. Stuart. 'The plant was watered in the ordinary way, and my father was so anxious to know whether the knife was rusting at all that he dug it up quite frequently. He was delighted when it stood that severe test.'

The three knives ... were tested in constant use from July 1914 to January 1916. One was used during that period by Mr. Stuart, the second by Mr. J. Tuffnell, and the third by Miss B. Froggatt, the last two persons being associated with Mosley and Co.

Sheffield Telegraph 26 March 1938 p 14

Harry Brearley also placed on record his gratitude: 'Mr. Ernest Stuart was at that time the cutlery manager at Messrs. R.F. Mosley's. It is due to him to say that from the very first trials he had confidence in the possibilities of the steel. He made unremitting efforts to adapt the process of knife-making to the unusual qualities of the steel.

'So far as the initial use of stainless steel for cutlery is concerned, Mosley's is the firm to whom credit is due.

'They looked well ahead; they did not expect too much of the steel; they realised that some improvements in appliances and skill in handling them were possible, and the excellent knives they produced justified their optimism. I am pleased to take this opportunity of thanking Messrs. R.F. Mosley for placing their works and Mr. Stuart's skill at my disposal. My relationship to their firm is simply that of an individual whose dream they realised after other too cautious counsellors had declared it to be a forlorn hope.' [2]

Ernest Stuart predicted a good future for stainless steel cutlery. Two months later he had ordered a total of 7 tons of steel from Amalgams Co, and would have liked a monopoly in the new material. Brearley referred all enquiries to Firth's and tried to interest them again in making special steel blanks to supply to cutlers, as then only ordinary cutlery processes would be needed to turn them into knives. His proposal was turned down, for Firth's were now claiming sole rights to the processes.

Promoting Rusnorstain

Well before their formal registration of the Rusnorstain trademark in Sheffield in 1924, Mosley's and in particular Ernest Stuart were promoting the name. Some of it led to fairly acrimonious newspaper articles and two can be seen in the Sheffield Telegraph of 4 February 1924: both an interview with Ernest Stuart and a response from Firth's to an article by Harry Brearley. However, we can say that the major facts are no longer in dispute.

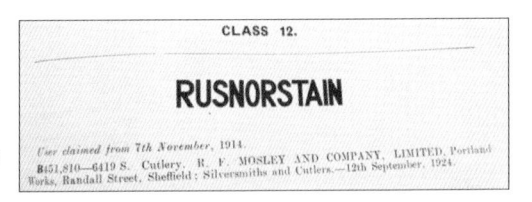

Ernest Stuart was a key person in the development of knives made of the new form of steel. He points out the hard work carried out by his firm to perfect the making of knives and corrects some common major objections – such as a remark that stainless steel is poisonous! It was not easy to accomplish during the 1914-18 war; the firm needed to use defective aeroplane valves as the raw material, for they were not allowed to buy the steel new. All supplies were needed for munitions.

Tribute was paid to the efforts of everyone who worked towards the success of the new product, including in the rejection of some faulty batches. Every batch had to be fully tested before use. 'Mr. A. O. Mosley, chairman and managing director of the firm, paid a glowing tribute to the experiments Mr. Stuart had done prior to the manufacture of stainless steel cutlery being made an accomplished fact. Even after stainless had become commercially possible Mr. Stuart did not for one moment relax his efforts to make the invention a complete success.'

The article also quotes one of the firm's workmen saying that the development days were very anxious, for 'we thought we should all land in the asylum, owing to the doubts of success'.

Regardless of extensive difficulties in obtaining the steel or selling the new stainless knives in this country, because World War 1 had started, Mosley's pressed ahead with sales to their established export markets in Australia. By October 1915 Rusnorstain cutlery was being promoted in the Australian press, such as the *Northern Star* of Lismore, NSW. By the end of the following year stockists included F Wicks, one of the premier jewellers in New South Wales, who had a reputation for selling items associated with 'the gorgeous East'.[3]

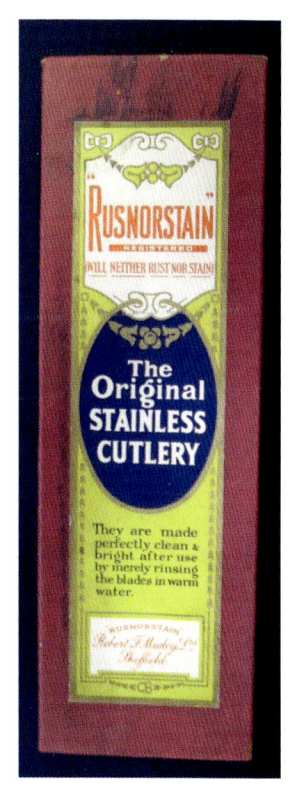

There was also a considerable 'puff' in the *Forbes Advocate*, NSW in September 1915. 'The beauty of these knives', it said, 'is that neither fruit, vinegar, nor any acid, nor exposure to the air will ever rust them. They merely need to be washed and dried from meal to meal, and they are ready for use.'

By February 1916 advertising had definitely got under way in England, for we traced an advert in the *Western Daily Press*, Bristol for the supply of cutlery by A Chillcott & Co. Later that year Mosley's were advertising in Sydney – such as in the *Evening News* on 20 October – and the adverts set a form which became familiar over the years.

In thanks for his work on Rusnorstain Ernest Stuart became a Director of Mosley's and was also (like several members of the Mosley family) a Freemason. He was initiated in 1919 at the age of 44 into St Leonard's Lodge, Surrey Street, Sheffield. Ernest made frequent trips to London on business, and stayed at the Russell Hotel, near the British Museum.

The trade name Rusnorstain

My thanks to Geoff Tweedale for much of the research on which this section is based; my apologies for the simplifications, made necessary by the tangled Brearley / Firth disputes.

Registration of Rusnorstain as a trademark is not easy to trace or to disentangle. There was some doubt at first whether the new steel worked, or whether it was actually a new material – and the advent of the first world war confused things. But we do have Brearley's constant story, which always gave credit to R F Mosley for the first use of the metal and the production, using it, of steel that would neither rust nor stain.

There is certainly evidence in Australian newspapers that Mosley was selling Rusnorstain knives there by the autumn of 1915. It is possible that Mosley's co-registered the mark in the USA around 1916, but it was apparently not until 12 September 1924 that they applied to register it in this country, according to official records held by the Company of Cutlers in Sheffield. The entry says that the company claimed use of the mark since 7 November 1914.

The registration also appears in the *Trade Marks Journal* for 19 August 1925 but it is elusive as the entry is indexed under Masley rather than Mosley. This index gives the registration address as Henry Hobson Mosley's home, 28 Grange Crescent, Sharrow, showing that after his father's death he was running the company.

'Rusnorstain' rather than 'stainless steel' was consistently used by Mosley's for most of the time that the company existed, although knives produced late in their history did sometimes use the latter mark. Even just before the company closed 'Rusnorstain' continued to be registered; the archive in the Cutlers' Hall has annotations showing how the mark was re-assigned after Mosley's finally went into liquidation.

R F Mosley's kept some of their earliest knives, and in 1938 three of the original batch, which had been tested by Stuart and two other people associated with Mosley's, were included in the American Exposition of Stainless Steel in New York, giving valuable publicity in an important new market. The story entitled *Three Old Knives Have Honoured Setting* can be found in the Sheffield Telegraph, 26 Mar 1938.

The Rusnorstain story continued. In 1929 Mr C Chamberlin of R F Mosley gave a talk in Whitstable, on the Kent coast, to the Canterbury and District Ironmongers' Assistants' Association. It was reported in the local newspaper, the *Whitstable and Tankerton Press*, on 2 November 1929 (page 5). He talked about the manufacture and care of cutlery but also told the story of stainless: 'After much trouble he [Mr Stuart] discovered an entirely new hardening and tempering process, which made cutlery of this steel a practical proposition. He produced, to Mr Brearley's delight, a dozen quite passable knives, which were distributed among their friends to be tested in use. These fulfilled expectations and stainless cutlery as a commercial proposition was launched.'

Ernest Stuart died on 16 April 1937 and is buried in Ecclesall Churchyard. The stainless steel crosses on the gravestone still shine today. His funeral was reported on 21 April in *The Daily Independent*; it was attended by a large number, including Masonic and business friends.

Prominent mention is made of the fact that Ernest was a pioneer of the development of stainless steel, and that he was a lifelong friend of Harry Brearley, its discoverer.

His gravestone states that buried with him are his wife Marie, also known as Annie, who died 3 August 1963, and his brother George (died 20 August 1928).

Pamela Stuart, 1926-2016

Ernest's son was Cyril Frederick (1902-1962), and he became cutlery manager at Mosley's after his father. In 1923 Cyril married Dorothy May Wheeler, who probably came from London - Dorothy was apparently a showgirl before their marriage. They had one child, Pamela, born on 21 November 1926. The marriage was not a happy one, and finally broke up. Dorothy and Pam moved into Collegiate Crescent. Pam always said they were poor, so this was maybe a rented flat in one of the houses of that road. Cyril had other relationships but never remarried.

After school Pam helped out at Portland Works, and remembered going to a workshop in the front range where blades were inspected and wrapped before the handles were put on.

During the Second World War the house on Ecclesall Road that had belonged to her grandfather Ernest was used as a school classroom, maybe for one of the schools damaged in the Blitz.

The involvement of Harry Brearley

His background

Brearley was the other key person in the story – the son of a worker in Thomas Firth's steelworks who was born in 1871. He was a self-taught man, for he intensely disliked the restrictions of formal schooling and left at the age of eleven. By 1883 he was twelve years old and could legally be employed at Firth's as a cellar-boy, his responsibilities being to carry beer for thirsty workers and to shovel coke.

Within a relatively short time he had proved himself to have an enquiring mind and, because he had a cleaner face than another boy, was offered a place in Firth's chemical laboratory. This gave him an even greater hunger for knowledge, and with the encouragement of the chief chemist he enrolled in evening classes and started to experiment in the laboratories – always looking for the experimental proof of what he was being taught. He continued to read, to experiment, and to explore the boundaries of his knowledge and skills all his life. He was capable and could have become an academic, but preferred to remain an experimental chemist and metallurgist.

It was in these years that Brearley, (right) with his brother-in-law, began work on a sideline – in 1903 they established a private metallurgical consulting practice researching composite materials and alloys. It grew over time to be the Amalgams Company which played an important role in later years. As just one example, in 1903 his short book 'The analytical chemistry of uranium' was welcomed as a clear explanation of its subject (as indeed it still is).[4]

In the following years he continued with 'numerous contributions to the literature of analytical chemistry'.

In 1904 he accepted a job as a chemist at a subsidiary of Firth's in Riga which made munitions, and later became works manager. He gained valuable experience in hardening materials within precise parameters. There he remained until 1907, when he returned to Sheffield in charge of Firth's new research laboratory. The Amalgams Company was thriving, and the interplay between Brearley's two interests sowed the seeds of much upset and conflict in later years.

Firth's offered Brearley a contract which included, as clause 8, a proviso giving sole rights in any of Brearley's discoveries to Firth's. Brearley objected, maintaining that 'morally, and perhaps legally, the discoverer was rightly the owner of his discovery.' So a new clause 8 was agreed: 'that new facts of commercial value discovered by me, or patents arising therefrom, should be the joint property of Firth's and myself. Further, if they [Firth's] bore the expenses of demonstrating the value of the said idea, costs of patents, etc., they should have the right to work such patents in their own works free of royalty.' Brearley was later advised that this clause had been badly drawn-up, and he admitted that he had probably been naive and too trusting. On the other hand, he and his family had been associated with Firth's for 60 years, and he believed that the company was honourable.

It worked for a while. Until 1913 Brearley worked for Firth's but also, and simultaneously, for the Amalgams Company. During that time Firth's took half the profit of a book that Brearley wrote, adhering to the terms of the revised clause 8.

Seeking a corrosion-resistant steel

In May 1912 the arms race which preceded the first world war was in full swing. The hunt was on for a new form of steel that would resist erosion and fouling in the barrels of rifles and larger armaments. Brearley (through the Amalgams Company) was asked by a small arms company to see if he could come up with such a material. He suggested some steels that he thought could do the job, and also that manufacturing and erosion trials could take place using an alloy of iron & chromium.

This was a difficult alloy to produce. By October 1912 batches of steel containing chromium had been made by the crucible process, but they proved not to be suitable. The experimenters turned to the electric furnace, and the second casting using this process proved successful, producing a steel with 0.24% carbon and 12.8% chromium. This metal seemed to resist erosion (though no-one suggested at the time that it might be stainless) and Brearley proposed that it be tested with a view for use as rifle barrels. However, it was extremely hard and difficult to work. Although it was resistant to etching by acids (including vinegar) there was no interest in using it for ordnance.

Brearley was left with a very hard, erosion- and acid-resistant form of steel for which there was no apparent practical use. He suggested cutlery as a possibility, but again none of the firms with which he was associated showed any interest. 'Nobody was impressed with my suggestion. Perhaps the idea of producing on a commercial scale a steel which should not corrode sounded ridiculous; at least my directors failed to grasp the significance of it.' He had a go himself, forging a knife blade and fitting it into the only handle available – one belonging to an old file. The result was not pretty, but Brearley said that he used it in his kitchen for years!

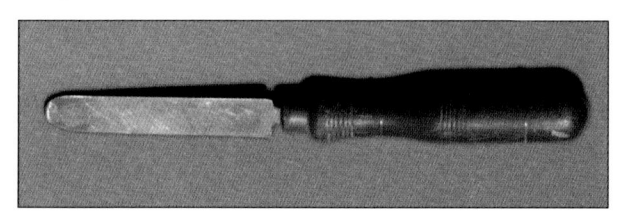

The very first stainless steel blade, made by Harry Brearley.

Brearley admitted that he probably made a nuisance of himself in the Firth's office, urging them to investigate this steel's usefulness for cutlery. At the end of 1913 Firth's sent samples to two Sheffield cutlers (without consulting Brearley) but the cutlers reported that the difficulties with forging, grinding and hardening were too great, and that they had made no viable knife blades. They lost interest again. Brearley knew that any would-be manufacturer needed his advice about the exact temperatures and processes for forging this steel, for it was very hard and brittle. One gets the impression that steel firms ignored the expertise on offer, reckoning that they were the experts and Brearley 'just' a chemist.

The Aftermath

By 1915 a long dispute over the terms of Brearley's contract had begun: 'It was assumed and at last plainly stated that I had no rights in the matter.' Brearley resigned from Firth's after a connection of 30 years. 'I left Firth's feeling that I had been wronged, and if I was not sorry I was sad.' Early in 1915 he started work as works manager of Brown Bayley's Steel Works, dealing mostly with munitions.

In the early days of his discovery of stainless steel Brearley did not seek to file for patents, as both its distinctive newness and its practical usefulness were in doubt. Thereafter, because of his dispute with Firth's, Brearley was unable to pursue patents in England. However in 1916, with the help of John Maddocks, a London man with contacts with America, a patent was granted in the USA.[5]

Firth's eventually bought a half-share in the American patent, and to give effect to the arrangement the Firth-Brearley Stainless Steel Syndicate was formed – theirs is the mark which appears on many knife-blades of the later 1920s and the 1930s. As part of the terms of their purchase Firth's agreed that they would no longer claim to be the original discoverers of stainless steel, but this restraint did not last. It was many years before the board of directors finally withdrew claims to

> I lunched with Mr. Brearley in Melbourne not long ago. When we sat down at a table he picked up a bread-and-butter knife and pointed to the trade-mark. 'You see,' he said, 'they lay my own knives for me wherever I go.'
>
> *Kalgoorlie Miner, 6* Sep 1930

have sole rights, and by then the damage to Brearley's reputation was done. Nevertheless, for all this time Mosley's made knives which did not stain, marked with their own tradename 'Rusnorstain'.

Brearley had to continue fighting for the rest of his life to be recognised as the chief discoverer of stainless steel – or at the very least the first person to find a commercial and viable use for it. He left examples of all the early production batches and a sealed letter with the Cutlers' Company, to be opened in 1960 in order to ensure that his story was not forgotten.

The original knife-mould, with an early knife laid in it
Photo taken by Will Roberts, May 2013

Since before the Rusnorstain story even began, Brearley had been living in Old Whittington, near Chesterfield – as the census entry in 1911 shows. Elmwood was the house of a prosperous man, with around 6 acres of land.

Later in his life he was awarded both the Bessemer Gold Medal and the Freedom of the City of Sheffield for his contributions to metallurgy. He retired in 1925 and, in bitterness, burned all his records a few years later. However, in 1941 he founded the Freshgate Trust to support endeavours in Sheffield. The Trust still exists, and Portland Works has been very grateful to receive repair grants from them.

Eventually Brearley moved to Torquay. He died there in 1948, but his brother Arthur and son Leo had died before him. His body was cremated and the ashes scattered in the crematorium garden of remembrance. The story is documented in Wikipedia.

Robert Fead Mosley

Robert Fead Mosley (RFM) is key to the history of Portland Works. The building was completed when he was in his late 30s, and by then he had already been in business in Sheffield for around 20 years. We need to find out a bit about his early life in order to understand him.

Robert was a London man – certainly his family had lived there for three generations, and quite possibly more. His grandfather Richard Mosley, who died in 1827, was a jeweller; his father Cornelius was born in 1812 and lived until 1885.[6] One cannot tell from black-and-white photos, but family members talk of RFM as a red-head; certainly a number of his descendants had red hair.

Childhood and beginnings

Cornelius and his wife Emma (nee Morgan) were married in London on 7 March 1835. The couple had 13 children, not all of whom lived to adulthood, and Robert Fead was their oldest surviving son. He was born in London on 23 August 1841, and baptised at the church of St Andrew, Holborn on 3 October 1841. The baptism record states that Robert's parents lived at 8 Hatton Garden, and that Cornelius was a jeweller.

In June of that year the 1841 census return reveals that Cornelius and Emma had three children older than Robert – they were Emma (5), Mary (4) and Albert (3).[7] Their children were mostly baptised at St Andrew's, but it is not clear if all survived childhood; certainly Albert died later in 1841. In the census Cornelius gave his occupation as a steel pen manufacturer, so his main occupation seems to have changed very recently. Steel pens were a recent innovation, coming into general use in the late 1830s; they were developed and manufactured by both cutlers and jewellers. Cornelius (sometimes known according to the records as Charles) and Emma continued to live at 8 Hatton Garden almost their entire lives.

Fead is unusual as a second forename, and was carried into future generations when it was given as a first name to Robert's grandson. Moreover, children named Fead seem always to have had Robert as their other name. It was pronounced 'Fade' and was evidently important to the family, but where did it come from? The only clue is that Robert's father Cornelius was executor (sole surviving executor when the time came) to the will of Caroline Fead, nee Hallifax, who died in 1862 and was the widow of Lt-Col George Fead CB. Fead had fought at Waterloo, and died in Woolwich in 1847.

Lt-Col Fead came from a military family - his father, also George, was a Lieutenant-General in the Royal Artillery, appointed Lieutenant-Governor of Port Royal, Jamaica in 1810, and had 9 sons, most of whom had military careers.[1] Neither George Fead mentioned anyone called Mosley in his will and I have not been able to trace any other connection between Cornelius Mosley and the Feads, other than a possibility that Cornelius and George may both have been members of the Freemasons in Edinburgh, before RFM's birth in 1841. Unfortunately baptism records at this date do not name the godparents, as this would seem a distinct possibility for the link. Alternatively we have to accept that Feads and Mosleys may have been social or business contacts at some point.

The next record of Robert's life is the 1851 census. We find him not at home in Hatton Garden with the rest of the family but already away at school, aged only 9. The school was The Grove, Milton, Gravesend – apparently a preparatory boarding school with 15 pupils. The head was a Yorkshireman, Mr Richard Trousdale, who lived in school with his wife, their 3 children and his sister. Other school staff named on the census were a teacher, a cook, a nurse and a housemaid. The youngest pupil was George Mosley, Robert's seven-year-old brother.

In 1856, after leaving school and at the age of only about 15, RFM went to work in Sheffield, as clerk in the office of George Oates, scissor manufacturer. Oates was originally from Loxley, just to the north-west of Sheffield, but then moved (possibly as the result of expansion) to the new Gatefield Works, on Robert Street near Infirmary Road. Robert Street no longer exists, but appears on late-nineteenth-century maps and ran parallel to Infirmary Road just north-west of the Infirmary Hospital. Gatefield House stands just south of Robert Street and presumably gave its name to the Works, which must still have been very new in 1856 for the whole area is still fields on a map surveyed in 1851.

Oates was a man of ideas, and in 1858 gave notice of his intention to file a patent for 'improvements in the manufacture of scissors'.[8] In 1861 his clerk Robert Mosley was living as a boarder in his house, which was in Upperthorpe, and named Bellmont. However, Oates died late in the same year. He left his money to his wife and daughters, and his business seems not to have survived, for it disappears from trade directories after this date.

All his household furniture and effects were advertised for sale by auction and they give an idea of his prosperous lifestyle.[9] His gold watch and watch-chain, and his set of gold studs, were considered worthy of a separate advertisement. The house contents, described in considerable detail, included not just the usual beds, chairs and tables but also Brussels carpets, a cottage pianoforte in rosewood, two 8-day clocks, furniture for five lodging-rooms, a shower bath and a 'sitz bath' (or hip bath), a large quantity of good quality tableware and kitchenware, and no less than 30 bottles of champagne!

However the young Mosley, aged only 20, now had neither a job nor an employer. Even at this young age he did not go back home, but immediately went into business on his own account. He was probably able to use the improved scissor process, and the story for the next fifteen years is one of expansion and diversification.

Growing the business

In 1863 Robert F Mosley is already listed as a scissor manufacturer in Brookhill – he continued doing what he was familiar with, but was not content with staying still. By 1864 he was not simply a scissor manufacturer, as he now made 'fine scissors, table cutlery etc' and was living in Sarah Street, just round the corner from his works premises at 214 Brook Hill (now demolished).[10]

Just before its demolition the works was almost certainly known as 'Cavendish Works', but it had had various names. In 1865 Kelly's names the premises as Highbury Works, Brook Hill, and in the autumn, in Islington, Robert married Martha Hobson of Highbury Hill, London.

Martha had been born in Sheffield and her parents were Henry and Ann (nee Pearce). Both had fathers who were Sheffield cutlery dealers. In 1841 Henry and Ann were about twenty, presumably newly-married, and living in Savile Street where Henry was a grinder by trade. By 1849

Henry had moved to London; according to the 1851 census he was living in Houndsditch and a hardware-man. In 1865 he appears on Robert and Martha's marriage certificate as a wholesale cutler.

It is probable that Henry gave (or lent) the young Robert a substantial sum of money upon his marriage – and that in gratitude, or in return, Robert named his works 'Highbury'. Marriage meant that Robert and Martha needed a family home; in 1868 the business is still listed at 212 Brookhill, but Mosley's home address is now in the newly-developed and prosperous road of Collegiate Crescent on the Broomhall Park Estate. He has definitely moved up in the world, and expansion seems to continue.[11]

Sadly Ann Hobson, Martha's mother, died in February 1869, leaving Henry with ten children younger than Martha, of whom seven were still living at home. It is maybe unsurprising that in 1870 Henry remarried, this time taking as his wife Kezia Stewart from High Barnet, Herts; she was ten years his junior and outlived him.

The entrepreneur takes off

In 1870 Robert Mosley was looking to move from his Brook Hill workshop to premises in West Street. The *Sheffield & Rotherham Independent* for 19 February 1870 prints an advertisement for a new tenant of his site, which shows that even his first solo business venture was not small: 'To be Let, on Lease or otherwise, a House, Warehouse and Workshops, now in the occupation of Mr. Robert Mosley, situate at 214, Brookhill and Sarah street, suitable for a Spring Knife Manufactory, or any other Light Business. – Apply, No. 2, Leicester street Foundry.' His move from Brook Hill to West Street was an advance in another way. Instead of leasing the premises, as seems to have been the case at Brook Hill, he became the freehold owner (see below).

In addition, Robert was thinking big, going international to sell quality goods. On Friday 9 June 1871 *The Argus* of Melbourne, Australia carried an advert for 'Superior Table Cutlery, R F Mosley's make, Sheffield' to be sold, apparently wholesale, to cutlers and ironmongers. He also added spring knives to the list of products.

By 1871 the works premises had moved to 188 West Street, known as the Beehive Wheel and shared with William Burkinshaw who was a woodturner. In the Sheffield of the day the term 'wheel' referred to a cluster of independent workshops which shared a common source of power; this would originally have been a waterwheel, but by the 1870s was more likely to be a steam engine.

Mosley was 29 and still living in Collegiate Crescent, with Martha (28) and their four children – Amy (4), Harry H (3), Lilian (2) and Robert Frederick (1). The house is identified as no. 19 (in the census) or Beech Dell (White's), and is either next to a small close called Beech Dell, or itself called Beech Dell – in either case it is still there on the south side, where there are shared drives leading to large houses behind the main building line. Robert was clearly doing well – also living in the house were four servants: a cook, a housemaid, a nurse and an undernurse.

1873 was a roller-coaster year for Robert and Martha Mosley. They seem to have been looking for a new house, possibly because they were expecting another child. Croft House came up for auction in late spring. The sale particulars (27 May 1873, with possession possible from June) suggest a recently-built house of high quality, with potential for the new owner both to have the accommodation extended into the attics to provide further bedrooms, and to buy additional land. The house was built in an acre of ground, which included a croquet lawn and shrub and rose gardens. Downstairs were a spacious entrance hall, dining, drawing and breakfast rooms, and two kitchens. Upstairs were six bedrooms, a bathroom and a WC. A selling point was that the house was a short distance from 'the stations of the Sharrow and Nether Edge Omnibuses, and commands an extensive view of Norton and the neighbourhood'. In common with house adverts today, the proximity of the Ecclesall Workhouse just down the hill is not mentioned, but almost certainly reduced the asking price.

Robert and Martha's next child, Alfred Gordon, was born on 22 August 1873 but a very terse announcement of his birth in the *Sheffield Daily Telegraph* the next day signals that all was not well. Alfred died very soon after his birth. Whether it was the loss of this child or the desire to have additional work done on Croft House we cannot know, but Robert and Martha seem not to have moved for a further year. Rutland Lodge, their house in Collegiate Crescent, was not advertised for let until 24 September 1874.[12]

In the midst of all this turmoil a partnership between Robert Mosley and Henry Lawton, cutlery manufacturers, was dissolved 'by mutual consent' in June 1873.[13] This seems not to have spoiled relationships between the Mosley and Lawton families, for Samuel Lawton was Mosley's table-knife manager for many years, and Arthur Lawton worked with Mosley from about 1870 until 1929.

Fatal accident

The steel and cutlery industries were hazardous. An incident was reported (as one of three Sheffield accidents that day) in the *Edinburgh Evening News* of 30 May 1873. 'Yesterday Thomas Twigg, 25, hammerman at Portland Works, Sheffield, while carrying a bar of hot iron on tongs, had to pass a steam hammer, which caught the tongs and thrust them against his breast, one of the tongs piercing his tongue. He was fearfully injured, and shortly afterwards died at the Infirmary.'

In the 1876 White's directory RFM is listed as a table cutlery and scissors manufacturer. His premises are now called Portland Works and are still in West Street; the Works was on the north side of West Street, next to Portland Lane. It is shown on the 1890 map and disappeared about 1900 when West Street was widened for electric trams. The handsome Cavendish Buildings of 1910 now fill this block.

This looks like further expansion and another move, but perusal of the directories shows that sometime between 1862 and 1879 West Street was renumbered. Just west of Portland Lane is the Beehive Hotel (surely the reason for the earlier name 'Beehive Wheel'). In 1862 the Beehive Hotel appears as 200 West Street, whereas in 1879 it remains in the same position but is numbered 240.

Mosley shared the works with George Gill, a spring knife maker – maybe he had passed the spring knife part of his business on to Gill.

By the spring of 1877 Mosley had decided to move premises again, as the West Street works was once more too small. It was put up for sale, and this time RFM is not a tenant for he owned the freehold.[14] The adverts show us a much larger works than the one in Brook Hill, in area about 862 square yards, 'consisting of a good dwelling-house and four large warehouses fronting West-street, with capital cellaring, three warehouses, and packing-rooms in the Yard. Also, numerous cutlers' workshops, eleven forging hearths, excellent grinding wheel with 36 light and heavy troughs, engine-house, and other buildings.' All machinery was also included in the sale, and other fixtures were to be bought by the purchaser at valuation; clearly the move to Randall Street was to be a fresh start, with all new and modern equipment.

Croft House: a secure family life

So by the time of the 1881 census we find the Mosley family well settled at Croft House. Robert was now, at the age of 39, a cutlery and silver plate manufacturer employing 240 people. Robert and Martha had three children at home (Amy, 14, Lilian, 12 and one-year-old Albert). Presumably their sons Harry and Robert were away at school. Visiting or living with them were Martha's father Henry and Robert's sister Alice. Their four domestic staff were now a cook, a parlour-maid, a nurse and a housemaid.

Further sadness came to the family in 1885; Robert's father Cornelius, now of 13 The Broadway, Streatham, but 'late of Hatton Garden' died in August at the age of 73, and was buried in Norwood Cemetery. When probate was granted to his wife and sole executrix Emma on 19 September 1885 he was described as a Gentleman, and his estate amounted to £432 10s. His will was very simple, for he left everything to Emma.

In 1887 Robert and Martha seem to have contemplated moving house, for Croft House is advertised in the press once more. They have improved the property – as well as the accommodation advertised in 1873 it boasts a conservatory leading from the drawing room, three rooms in the attic, and outbuildings including a stable, coach-house and greenhouses.[15] Maybe they could not find a buyer, or perhaps they could not find another house they liked - for whatever reason, they stayed in Croft House.

By 1891 Robert and Martha's children were mostly adults, though still living at home. Amy, the eldest, was 24 and her sister Lilian 22; neither has an occupation given in the census return. Henry H (23) and Robert F (21) are 'learning the business of cutlery manufacture' while Albert O (11) is still at school. The family still have four domestic servants – a cook, a housemaid, a parlourmaid and an under-parlourmaid.

In 1891, too, we find that Henry and Kezia Hobson had moved to Sheffield, and were living at 'Lyndhurst' on Rutland Park.

Henry Hobson died on 29 July 1897, and was buried alongside his first wife in Highgate Cemetery 'in the grave ... purchased by me in 1869'. He directs that any of his children who die unmarried may be buried in the same grave. The will, dated 5 November 1896, reveals quite a lot about his family and his loyalties. Henry names ten equal inheritors: his son George Frederick Hobson; the children of 'my late son Henry Hobson'; and eight daughters - Martha Ann Mosley, Alice Pearce

The Hobson and Mosley families about 1890. Martha Mosley (nee Hobson) is seated in the middle; Robert stands on the far left, with Lilian to his left and Amelia in front of them. Albert is up the tree. Behind Martha is her father Henry Hobson with his wife Kezia beside him. Others in the photo are members of the Hobson family.

Hobson, Fanny Webster, Florence Gilson, Ada Thompson Gidney, Emily Holroyd Maxfield, Amelia Daw, Marian Hobson. We can deduce that their eleventh child Alfred had died before his father.

Henry names as his executors his surviving son George Frederick Hobson (cutlery merchant) and three sons-in-law: Robert Fead Mosley (manufacturer), William Thomas Gidney and Frank Webster.

He left to his 'dear wife Kezia' (among other things, including £200 of ready cash to keep her going while his affairs were wound up) 'my portrait in oil by Turner of Barnsbury'.[16] He also directs that money invested by his Trustees in the process of distribution may be invested in any of a long list of specified stocks and shares in Great Britain. It specifies particularly that investments may be made in 'any Company which may be formed in relation to the business of R F Mosley & Co'.

Henry Hobson, d1897

The grant of probate on 12 October refers to him as a Gentleman, of 'Lyndhurst', Rutland Road, Sheffield. His estate was considerable, amounting to £42,612 14s 5d. Kezia lived nearly another fifteen years, until 1912; she died on 2 July back 'home' in Barnet.

The 1901 census reveals that Robert and Martha are in their late 50s and have only Albert (21) living at home. Both Robert and Albert are described as 'cutlery and electroplate white manufacturer'. They had four domestic servants still, and also a nurse. This could well imply that someone in the house needed attention, and it is possible this was Albert, who suffered ill-health all his life.

Ten years further on, the 1911 census tells us a little more about the house: it has 13 rooms (including the kitchen but excluding landing, bathroom, scullery etc) so is a large one. Robert and Martha are now in their late 60s and have been married for 45 years. They have had a total of six children, of whom five are still alive. And they still have a cook and two housemaids.

The house still exists and is indeed large, at the very top of Lyndhurst Road. Robert died there in 1921.

This photograph, taken in about 1908-1910, shows Portland Works in 'another guise' – as Alexander Clark's 'Welbeck Works'. It was the association between Mosley and Clark which gave the Works its true heyday. For the postman, things addressed differently but for the same place must have been confusing. This is further explored in the next chapter.

Heyday - a vision of excellence

Portland Works

The trade directory for 1879 shows that Mosley is now established at the newly-built Portland Works in Randall Street. He has both business premises and a home which will last him for the rest of his life. The trade directories state that he is a manufacturer of table cutlery, scissors, pen and pocket knives etc. The 1881 census fills in the further detail, that of his 240 employees twenty are boys and twenty are girls.

    The whole area between Bramall Lane and London Road was fields and gardens in 1863. By 1873 Hill Street and Randall Street were laid out, but few buildings had been constructed. In the late 1870s the area was developed with shops, housing and works. In the same 'block' are John Street Works (silver), Randall Street Steam Joinery and Moulding Works, and Nelson Works (steel and files). Portland Works and John Street Works (which adjoins at the back and is now known as Stag Works) were both designed by J H Jenkinson and built in 1877.[17] John Street Works was occupied by Henry Wigfull, a silver manufacturer who had moved from the same area as Mosley near West Street, his previous base being known as the Charlotte Street Works. One begins to see patterns of friendship and association as these entrepreneurs develop their businesses.

    A little snippet from 1884 may show us that while he established the cutlery business further, RFM also provided a base for people who were building up the firm. On 19 Jan 1884 an advert in the Independent reveals that Horton Bros (originally George and William, born in Birmingham) had gone out of business – they were auger makers trading at Wright's Hill, Highfield with a very small workforce. Their equipment was sold off, and the first hour of the auction was held at Portland Works in Hill Street, where the Hortons had presumably been working.

    We have an illustration from a book of 1888, and the map of 1889 which clearly show the same building as the one which existed about 1920. This post-war image is seen on the invoice on the next page. You can see the archway, the chimney, the central block in the yard, and three storeys on the rear and right-hand ranges. This was an early purpose-built, integrated cutlery factory, where all processes happened under one roof. As such it was something of an innovation, and showed that Mosley was keeping in with new developments as the industry grew.

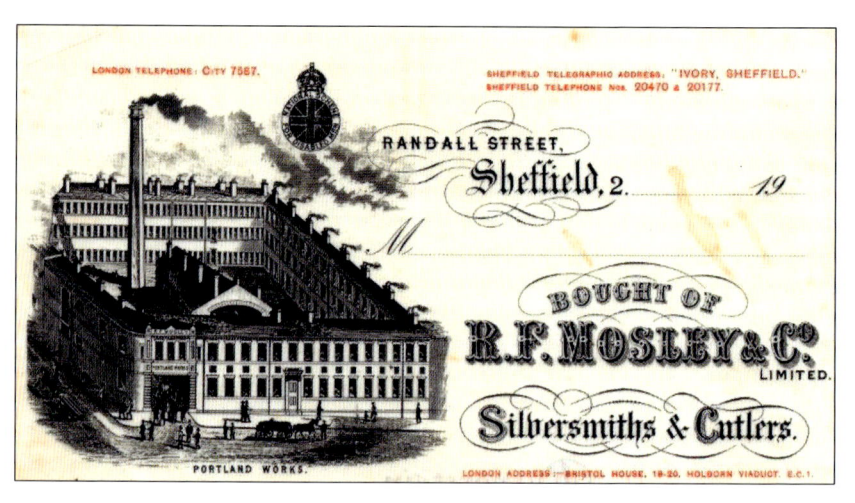

Up to now, people in separate workshops had moved products from place to place as the knives were made. Now, even if some of the workers were self-employed and rented a workshop, the entire process happened on one site. Steel bars came in, finished goods went out. Mosley continued to share the works; George Gill came with him from West Street, and was now listed as a cutlery manufacturer, but he left by 1881. William H Green continued to make spring knives.

Why Mosley gave the new Works the same name as his former base (which continued to exist) is not known, but was possibly to keep the flow of communication to the firm intact. In 1883 Mosley registered a Sheffield silver mark so he was continuing to expand and moving into silver, a sign of quality products, as well as cutlery. Around 1887 a publicity article said of Mosley's: 'A valuable feature of their business, and one which has been made a speciality by them, is the manufacture of case goods on an exceedingly artistic and extensive scale. These cases are fitted up with satin and velvet linings, etc., for the reception of cutlery of the best and highly finished kinds, also for silver dessert and table spoons, forks, fish knives, etc., mounted in pearl, ivory, silver, metal and other choice mountings.'[18]

The obituary of C W Kayser in 1906 gives us a glimpse of Mosley's reputation by the 1880s, when he had just moved to Randall Street. Charles William Kayser was a German man who settled in Britain, but on his first visit to England he wanted to study the Sheffield cutlery and steel trades. His obituary says that he 'was a scissorsmith, and in this capacity obtained employment with the firm of R.F. Moseley [sic] and Co., Randall Street.' There he perfected his English, decided to remain in England, and started moving to other companies. By the time of his death he was one of the greatest living authorities in crucible steel manufacture. In addition 'One son, Mr C.W. Kayser, is a director of Kayser, Ellison, and Co. (Limited), and the other, Mr. Frank Kayser, is a director of the Austin Motor Co. (Limited), Birmingham'[19]

I have been able to look at very few company records, and mentions in the press are few and hard to find – probably quite a good sign. But here is one, of a strike by Sheffield hafters who wanted a 10% pay increase. Mosley was one of the employers resisting the strike, but eventually had to give in.

Table and Butchers' Knife Hafters

For some time there has been a movement amongst the table and butchers' knife hafters for an increase to wages. Some firms granted an advance of 10 per cent, but others refused. Amongst the latter were Messrs. R.F. Mosley and Co., Portland Works, Randall street, and as a result between 50 and 60 men came out on strike about six weeks' ago. At the same time nearly twenty grinders made a similar demand, and also stopped work. The matter has since been considered by both parties, and yesterday the men were informed that the 10 per cent advance would be conceded. The dispute is therefore at an end.

Sheffield Daily Telegraph 16 Aug 1890

There are also a few references to industrial accidents – but they were common in such an industrial city, and merited only a few lines. The worst were caused by grinding wheels shattering and flying apart, but there were also scalds and crushing injuries.

White's Directory of 1901 shows that R F Mosley & Co Ltd, cutlery manufacturers, are sharing Portland Works with W Mammatt & Sons, electro plate manufacturers, and J T Johnson & Sons, steam joinery manufacturers. Mammatt's seem to have been expanding in the late 1890s. Adverts in the Sheffield Telegraph in August 1897 show that they were looking for 'a good General Chaser, one preferred with assistant' and 'two or three good Metalsmiths, must be well up in all branches'. That is, up to five extra experienced staff all at one time.[20]

The next stage of our story shows Robert Mosley continuing to develop his capacity to produce high-class products for a wide market, but without needing to put his own name on all that he made.

Partnership with Alexander Clark

Clift Alexander Mawer Clark had been born London in 1857, the son of Alexander Clark, an accountant. When he married Caroline Elizabeth Stocker on 17 August 1881 Clift and both the fathers were described as 'Gentleman' so we can assume his upbringing was comfortable. He was known in business circles as Alexander Clark.

By 1891 he and his family were living in Avenue Villa, Cavendish Road, Sutton, Surrey and his occupation as 'manager of a warehouse' led to them being comfortably-off. He also had a business as a 'dressing bag, portmanteau, purse and empty bag maker, silversmith & cutler' at 138 Fenchurch Street, and in 1894 opened his works (also Portland Works) and a shop at Market Place, close to Oxford Street.

When RFM's son Robert Frederick left home after learning the cutlery trade he moved to London, to 29 Market Place – very close to Clark's Market Place works. By 1901 he had married Margaret Lucy Jones and they had started a family. Clark had also moved, to Holland Road, Sutton, where his house was called 'Brincliffe' – the area of Sheffield where Mosley lived. It is clear that the Mosleys and Clark were friends and in business together. Alexander is described as a manufacturing silversmith; he and Carrie, his wife, have 5 children (including son Vernon, now 18 and a silversmith's assistant) living at home.

The real money in the trade from about the 1880s was in silver (mostly electroplated) cutlery and other tableware, not in pocket knives, Bowies etc. One only had to look at the fortunes generated by the Mappins etc, who recognised the importance of this market and the money to be made if you could get plugged into the London market. Mosley moved into his bigger premises at exactly that time – with space for silversmiths and electroplating – yet he seemed never to advertise in his own right until the 1920s. But the Clark connection shows that he did not need to.

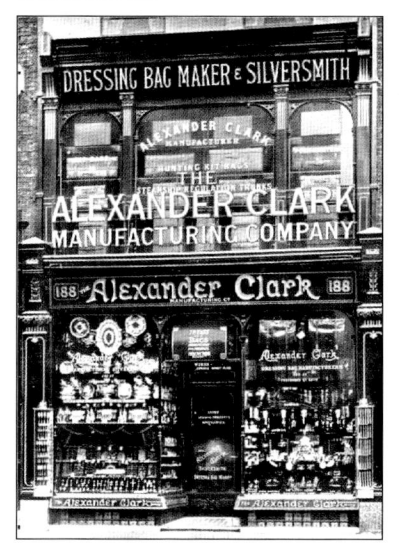

Clark's was no backstreet shop. It was Mosley's alter ego - and vice versa. The shop (left) was in Oxford Street, London, a few doors away from Mappin & Webb's. It was large, and had at least three floors.

Early in the 1900s we find statements that the manufacturing of silverware for Clark's business was now located at Welbeck Works in Randall Street (below). It is clear that, as Clark already had a 'Portland Works' in London, making bags and portmanteaus, he re-named the Portland Works in Sheffield – but only as far as his own catalogues and his own contacts were concerned. And, of course, it affected the postman – who now had not only to distinguish between the old Portland Works on West Street and the newer one on Randall Street, but also had to remember that post for Welbeck Works also needed delivering to the newer Portland Works building!

By 1906 the directors of the company were listed as Alexander Clark and Robert Frederick Mosley and the firm was active at both 29 Market Place and 188 Oxford Street in London. By 1910 there were two further partners, Robert Fead Mosley and Louis Vernon Clark, son of Alexander. That year the entry in the London Post Office Directory, under Cutlers, reads:

Alexander Clark Manufacturing Co: 125 & 126 Fenchurch St, EC; 8 & 9 Fen ct EC; & 188 Oxford St W; manufactories Portland Works, 29 Market Pl W; & Welbeck silver plate & cutlery works, Randall St & Hill Street, Sheffield.

Silversmiths, from Clark's catalogue
This workshop is in the basement at Portland Works

Alexander Clark's company had some stupendously wealthy customers, and Mosley's company provided him with a ready-made manufacturing arm, supplying orders of silver and cutlery. Some of these were huge. For example, in 1899 there was an official query over hallmarking. R F Mosley's firm was making for Alexander Clark 'a complete dinner service for twenty-four persons, every article being made in sterling silver and elaborately decorated in repoussé, after the style of Louis XIV.' This had been ordered by Alexander Clark of 188 Oxford Street, London and the final purchaser was to be a Government official in Mecca, who was preparing to entertain the Sultan of Turkey during the summer.

It was no small order, but whose hallmark should be on it? This was a substantial question to ask, for the total weight of silver used was 'between 5,000 and 6,000 ounces, and it is calculated that the cost to the purchaser, including a number of oaken plate chests, will exceed £3,000.'[21] The weight in ounces is hard to visualise – but 5,500 ounces is approximately 150 kg (or 25 stone) of silver! Unfortunately we do not know what answer was given.

This was not the only large order for Clark, for he was also a retailer of jewellery and gems. Some idea of the scale of his company can be gained from a report of an incident, a jewel heist, which occurred in October 1907. The R F Mosley in question was Robert Frederick, who was working with Clark in London. On a night-train train from London to Naples Robert was robbed of diamonds worth $1,000 as well as $350 in cash. He was taking a quantity of jewels (not for the first time) to the King of Siam. Fortunately the majority of the jewels were not stolen. A newspaper reports what Mosley said about the night-train incident:

'I took a return ticket from London to Rome, in order to take a special selection of the finest jewelry *[sic]* for the King of Siam's inspection … I asked for a bottle of soda water soon after starting, and as I had no small change, pulled out a bundle of notes - $225 English and $125 Italian and French. The attendant gave me change for one of the notes, and I put the others back in the inside pocket of my coat, where I also had $1,000 worth of loose diamonds.

'Before going to sleep I hung up my coat, waistcoat and trousers on a hook. The thieves, who had evidently seen me put away the notes, stole the coat and waistcoat during the night, but fortunately did not touch the trousers, in the hip pocket of which were $10,000 worth of loose jewels, mostly diamonds and emeralds. In my suit case I had from $30,000 to $40,000 worth of mounted gems.'[22]

Mosley reported the incident on reaching Naples. One of the train attendants was immediately arrested and the police were optimistic about recovering the distinctive jewels. On his return to England he was told that his movements had been watched ever since a previous trip to Berlin.

The partnership became a limited company (as Alexander Clark Co

Ltd) in 1912, with Alexander Clark and Robert Fead Mosley as the two directors.

About that time the Alexander Clark Manufacturing Co Ltd said it employed 620 people in all – cutlers, silversmiths, precious stone mounters and dressing bag manufacturers. It specialised in the production of silver, 'Welbeck' silver plate and electroplate, cutlery, fitted dressing cases and bags, and high-class leather goods. Silver plate trademarked 'Welbeck' was guaranteed for no less than thirty years, in itself showing its quality.

R F Mosley in his garden, about 1910. I have found no photos of Clark.

The business was clearly doing well, for by 1911 Clark had moved house again, to Westwood, New Hill, Sydenham, where he was living in a substantial 16-roomed house with his wife Cary, son Leigh (21 and a silversmith's assistant), daughter Elsie and two servants. In 1918 he also had a manufacturing presence in Birmingham, and by 1921 the business had further addresses at 38-40 Mitre Street, Aldgate, London and 17 Sycamore Street, Sheffield (which ran parallel to Norfolk Street, where the Crucible Theatre now stands). Alexander Clark was among the mourners at Mosley's funeral in 1921, when the two men were reported to have been in partnership for 18 years (ie since 1903) but evidence clearly shows that the business relationship may well have been longer than that.

Publicity for 'Welbeck Plate' in Clark's catalogue

Around 1908-1910 Alexander Clark & Co produced more than one version of a lavishly illustrated catalogue. I have seen two editions of the catalogue, both undated, and it is worth pointing out that one or more of the photos that are clearly and correctly of the Sheffield works in one version claim to have been taken at James Street, Birmingham in the other! It is remarkable that Clark guaranteed his 'Welbeck' Plate, which Mosley's would have made, for a full thirty years.

Among the illustrations are several showing his Sheffield works – some of which are to be found throughout this book. They clearly show hand-drawn 'post-production' lettering on the buildings, declaring the premises to be 'Welbeck Works – The Alexander Clark Manufacturing Co'. Unfortunately when you look closely the lettering goes over the guttering, rather than behind! It was the Edwardian equivalent of digital picture editing, and shows that even then the camera could lie. A further example is 'the Showroom' – which could be an entire fabrication below the line of the ceiling and its trusses! We have definitely identified the room at Portland Works, but there are no shadows, and both the details and the perspective are wrong ...

One of the pictures that is almost certainly 'good' is that of the hand-forges, (block B on the map), shown above. They now have glazed windows, but a few doors are still two-part 'stable-type in design. The Sheffield 'Pevsner' (by Harman and Minnis) says they are among the best-preserved in England.

Regardless of any difficulties in selling the new stainless knives in this country, Mosley's pressed ahead with their established export markets.

By October 1915 Rusnorstain cutlery was being promoted in the Australian press.[23] The following year stockists included F Wicks, one of the premier jewellers in New South Wales, who had a reputation for selling items associated with 'the gorgeous East'.[24] Possibly the contact had been made because of Clark's trade with the King of Siam.

When describing silver made by Alexander Clark and Co, auction sites on the internet sometimes mention that one of his major suppliers was R F Mosley and suggest that this is one reason why there is so much silver marked 'Clark' compared to that marked 'Mosley'. It seems certain that it suited both men to work closely together, while maintaining separate identities for their businesses in public. Mosley got a prestigious London outlet where his son worked, and Clark had a close relationship with an important Sheffield supplier, while neither 'lost' their own business. It seems likely that this arrangement lasted until 1938, when Clark died.

Fish knife with a blade marked with 'Alex Clark Co Ld, Welbeck'

Clark died on 25 September 1938 at Elliotts, Nuthurst, Sussex. He left an estate valued at £44,939 8s 3d and the trustees of his property were his son Vernon (by then a jeweller) and his daughter Doris.

Other connections

In Kelly's Directory for 1934 we see three listed occupants of Portland Works. There is R F Mosley & Co Ltd, cutlery manufacturer, alongside Clark Company Ltd (The Alexander Cutlery Works) and John Thomas Johnson & Sons, steam manufacturing joiners. By now Johnson's had been co-tenants for at least 30 years, and it seems reasonable to assume that they made all Mosley's cutlery cabinets.

Evidence from the Works

In a few places around the Works we have found dating evidence for alterations that were made to expand the space. One example is a piece of newspaper, severely scrunched-up, which was used to fill a hole in the wall before it was re-plastered. The hole was left by the demolition of a cross-wall to give access to newly-added rooms behind the entrance, and the newspaper's date is Thursday 29 December 1892. So the work is likely to have taken place at the start of 1893.

Portland Works 'finishing room' in about 1908.
This room is restored and in use as our 'Makerspace'

West End connections

However, life did not all revolve round the Works! As early as 1887 one of the R F Mosleys living at Croft House had prominent connections with the London theatre, revealed by a letter written by Frederick Leslie, connected to the theatre scene. It was addressed from Croft House, and appears in a London weekly newspaper, *The Era*, as part of publicity for a production at the Gaiety Theatre, Strand.[25] It congratulates Mr George Stone for his performance as Gringoire in *Miss Esmeralda*. This play was a melodrama written by Frederick Leslie himself (the pen name of A C Torr) and Horace Mills, with songs by Robert Martin, and *The Era* was a newspaper with a strong focus on theatrical affairs.

The Lawton Family

The Lawton family worked with and for the Mosleys for many years, but the details of quite how they related to each other is not easy to discover. The *London Gazette* tells us on 7 November 1873 that R F Mosley and Henry Lawton dissolved a partnership, by mutual consent.

A Henry Lawton (who may or may not be the same person) died in 1885 on his way to New Zealand; his will was administered by his son (a grocer) and by his nephew Arthur of 24 Upper Hanover Street, a table knife manager. It is possible that this Arthur is the same man who appears in the 1911 census. He was 55, had been married to Solina for 32 years and was a manufacturer of fish eaters.

We are on firmer ground with the next entry, who could again be the same person. In 1929 Arthur Lawton retired after 60 years working for R F Mosley, but remained a director of the company – a position he had apparently held for 20 years. The report of his retirement holds a mini-history of the company: 'When Mr. Lawton entered the service of the firm at the age of ten, the business was conducted in Sarah Street, and the employees numbered between 20 and 30. Later the firm removed to West Street, and in 1877 premises were built in Randall Street. In his younger days Mr. Lawton worked daily from 8.30 a.m. to 8 p.m. Mr. Lawton's father was connected with the business for a number of years, and Mr. Lawton's son, who has had 34 years' service with the firm, is now the secretary.' As well as his business interests Arthur tended his garden, had been president of the Hallamshire Bowling Club, and had 'a fine collection' of water-colour paintings.

The end of R F Mosley's era

Mosley the man

The bare bones of official records tell us little about Mosley as a person, but it is possible we can glean something from family stories, as well as a little from official documents such as census returns, for he seems to have been a 'good' employer.

In an age when many servants endured poor conditions and ill-treatment, relatively few stayed in the same domestic job for long. Yet people were apparently happy to have more than one member of the family working as servants in the Mosley household. In 1871 Harriet Hessell was a housemaid and Fanny Hessell the nurse; in 1881 we find Charlotte Richardson as cook and Harriett Richardson as housemaid. Moreover Mary Stubbings (or Stubbins) seems to have stayed with the Mosleys for over 20 years; she was a parlourmaid in 1881 and 1891, and still with them in 1901. By 1891 there was also a younger member of the Stubbins family (Alice), who was Mary's under-parlourmaid. Their housemaid Elizabeth Ibbotson appears in the 1901 census and was still with them in 1911. It seems reasonable to interpret this long-term loyalty as evidence that Robert and Martha were good employers – possibly kind and considerate, as well as paying a fair wage.

Mosley's business career adds to the impression given by the loyalty of his domestic staff that he was a man that it was good to work with and for. When he moved to Portland Works he took with him George Gill, who had shared the previous premises, and he seems to have been good at delegating certain parts of his processes to others, starting with spring knives.

As his business grew he developed strong and lasting links with Alexander Clark, who made both Robert Mosleys (father and son) directors of his firm. He gave Ernest Stuart the freedom to experiment with Brearley's steel, bringing further opportunities to the company. Robert Mosley never seems to have wanted to claim all the credit for his work that he could have done: he supplied knife blades and silver for Alexander Clark, and he did not push for recognition of his role in developing stainless steel knives. That is the attitude of a man with a natural humility and gentleness.

Robert Fead Mosley died on 13 January 1921, at the good age of 79. He was interred in the family vault at Fulwood; for his funeral the church was crowded, with about 420 mourners and employees. All three sons and two grandsons (Geoffrey Davis and Robert Clive Mosley) were present, as well as representatives of the firm including: 'Messrs A Lawton, senior; Stuart; Chamberlain; Kirkby (directors); A Lawton, junior (secretary); Bullard from the London Office; Smith; Ashley; Lees; Marsden; Cocker and Tufnell.' Others present included Messrs Seligman, W Holmes, P Richard, A T Capewell, Alexander Clark (London, partner of the late Mr Mosley for 18 years), Tom Bowler, Albert Lee, Samuel Lawton, Fead Lawton, Arthur Beardshaw, Benjamin Wigfull, Joshua Wigfull, William David and Mrs Pollitt.

The press went on to say that the coffin was borne by six workmen, whose combined years of service with the firm numbered 270, with an average of 45 years. They were Messrs Tom Reaney, Mark Reaney, John Redfearn, Robert Smith, Thomas Shillito and Herbert Gregory.

Mosley the man, the employer, had kept the loyalty of ordinary people, his workers, whose average length of service was sufficiently long to merit special mention. His family is what matters on the memorial inscribed below a cross over his grave in Fulwood churchyard.

> In loving memory of
> ROBERT FEAD MOSLEY
> Croft House, Brincliffe
> who passed peacefully away on
> Jan the 13th 1921, aged 79 years.
> Also of
> MARTHA ANN MOSLEY
> wife of the above
> who passed peacefully away on Nov 5th 1926
> in her 85th year.

Let that memorial speak for itself.

Mosley's legacy

For the family Robert Mosley's legacy would have concerned his property and his will as well as the business. The executors were his sons - Henry Hobson Mosley of 28 Grange Crescent, Sharrow, cutlery manufacturer, Robert Frederick Mosley of Albemarle Street, Middx, jeweller and silversmith, and Albert Oswald Mosley of 132 Psalter Lane, Sheffield, cutlery manufacturer.

Robert left his estate in trust to his wife Martha, for her lifetime, and after her death to his children in equal shares, but gave no further names or details in his will. Probate was granted on 15 April 1921 and the value of the estate was £52,966 7s 9d. Martha survived him, and died towards the end of 1926. It is hard to grasp how very wealthy Robert was – one indication is that on the page in the probate register giving brief details of his estate there are 34 entries; Robert leaves by far the largest estate; next is one of £19,266 and there are only 8 others over £1,000 (the largest being £6,347). So 24 of the 34 people left estates of less (usually considerably less) than £1,000.

Yet there is another legacy. It was Robert Mosley who developed from scissor manufacturer into innovative cutlery maker, and who invested heavily in the building of Portland Works, one of the earliest integrated metal workshops in Sheffield. There steel could be taken from forging, through its various processes of grinding, assembling and polishing right through to wrapping, assembling in cabinets and boxes and distributing.

It was he who gave permission for Portland Works to be the venue for experimentation with the new chromium steel alloy. It was he who allowed the tests to continue even after 'adjectival stamping tools' had been broken during the first attempt. It was he who would have liked the freedom of a monopoly in the metal to allow him to take innovation further, but was for various reasons unable to obtain one.

The next generation

What of Robert's children, what became of them? And what happened to the business? All three sons were executors of their father's will in 1921, but there were also two daughters. We will leave the youngest son, Albert, for a moment, but here is something about the other children.

Henry Hobson Mosley (the oldest child, born 1867) married Edith Emma Greenwood on 29 March 1893 at St Mary's, Stoke Newington, London. He was 25 and a cutler; Edith was 27 and the daughter of Henry George Greenwood, accountant. The witnesses were William Greenwood and (quite unusually) two others, both female - Lilian Mosley and Amy Davis, who were Henry's sisters. By 1901 Henry and his family were living at 28 Grange Crescent, Sharrow. He was 33 and a spring knife cutler / cutlery manufacturer. His wife Edith was 36 and they had three daughters – Edith G (6), Vera (5) and Katholine (3); there were also three servants – a governess, a nurse and a general servant. They were still living there in 1911 so we know that the house had 8 rooms and that they had been married for 18 years, having had 3 children all of whom were still living; the girls are now named in full as Edith Gwendoline (16), Vera (15) and Catholeen (13).

Henry had always worked for his father, and it was presumably expected that he would carry on the business for several years at least. However, Henry unfortunately fell ill and gave up work. In fact he was more-or-less an invalid for the last five years or so years of his life, but we have no details of his illness. He died at home on 12 March 1928, leaving an estate worth £4,829 12s 6d to be administered by his widow Edith Emma and his brother Albert Oswald. The *Sheffield Daily Telegraph* on Tuesday 13 March 1928 reported:

> 'The death occurred yesterday on Mr. Henry Hobson Mosley, of 28, Grange Crescent, Sheffield. Mr. Mosley, who was in his 61st year, was a director of the well-known firm of Messrs. R. F. Mosley and Co., Ltd., cutlery manufacturers, of Randall Street, Sheffield, who were the first to make cutlery from stainless steel. He was the elder son of the late Mr. R. F. Mosley, founder of the firm, with which he was associated practically all his life. For several years, however, he had been an invalid. He leaves a widow and three daughters. Although he took no part in any public work, he was respected for generous philanthropy.'

The funeral was held a few days later, at Ecclesall Church. As well as family mourners those in attendance included Arthur Lawton, A D Kirkby, Ernest Stuart and Donald Chamberlain (all directors of the company) as well as other business contacts.

Robert Frederick Mosley, the second son, was commonly known as Bobby. He had married Margaret Lucy Jones of Sheffield in early 1895 and they set up home in Sheffield. However, by April 1896 they were on the move, for on 24 March the Sheffield Telegraph advertised that their house on Grange Crescent Road was to let 'in about a month'.

The move was to London, for Bobby was working closely with Alexander Clark (see the previous chapter) and seems to have been very successful. According to the 1901 census they were living at 29 Market Place in the parish of All Saints' Margaret Street. Bobby was 33 and a gold jeweller; his wife was 34. They now had a two-year-old son, Robert Fead Mosley, born in 1898, and two live-in servants.

Soon after his father's death Bobby apparently cut down what he was doing, possibly to give more time to the base in Sheffield. A notice appears in The London Gazette on 5 April 1921 that a partnership has been dissolved between Robert Frederick Mosley and Arthur Samuel Flowers, carrying on business as Jewellers, at 1A, Albemarle-street, as 'Mosley, Flowers & Co'.

However, Bobby also died young, in 1926. His death came at a hotel in Beaulieu, France, on 19 January 1926 – in south-western France. Probate was granted to his younger brother Albert; his estate was valued at £2,850. Little is known about his death – for instance, did he simply happen to be at the hotel? Or, as seems possible from its location, was he yet another member of the family who had fallen gravely ill, and convalescing there?

It seems likely that Bobby carried an interest in theatre with him when he went to London, and passed it on to his own son. The youngest Robert seems to have been much less of an astute businessman than his grandfather. While his father was still alive he had formed, and dissolved, a partnership with Lionel Harris as theatrical managers and agents and this failed venture appears to have led to his bankruptcy in 1921. He must have been a considerable worry to his grandfather, who was already nearly 80 and in the last few months of his life. He was eventually discharged from bankruptcy on 9 March 1923, having agreed to pay £1 10s to the Official Receiver.

Robert and Martha's **elder daughter Amy** lived at home until she married, on 30 March 1892, Frederick Pittman Davis at St Andrew's, Sharrow. The ministers were two Hobson uncles, Revd W T Gidney and Revd H R Gidney. It was probably a fairly quiet wedding, for the notice in the newspaper requested 'no cards'. From the account of her father's funeral we gather that they had at least one child, for Geoffrey Davis (grandson) is named as a mourner, but I have uncovered little else.

WW1 - Richard Henry Valentine Hoskings, 1896 - 1917

The outbreak of war late in 1914 gave Sheffield's cutlery industry major problems, both in sourcing materials and in sales. This is one example of the human cost - Richard and Edwin worked for Mosley's before the war.

Richard came from Exmouth, but moved with his family to Sheffield when he was about 5. By 1911 Richard and his brother Edwin were working at Portland Works. In 1914, possibly before the start of the war, Richard enlisted as a private in the King's Own (Yorkshire Light Infantry). Edwin tried to enlist, but was rejected because of illness.

Richard did not serve overseas until 1916 but then he served in several battalions and by 14 April 1917 was in the 34th Division of the British Fourth Army. That spring he fought in the First and Second Battles of the Scarpe and the actions on the Hindenberg Line (all in the Arras area). Then after some rest and recuperation, he was again in action and pinned down for 48 hours.

At last he got some proper rest, in a camp 25 miles from Arras – entertainment and sport along with things like assault courses and training. In June 2017 they were back in the trenches and on the front line. During the evening of 5 June their attack began with a barrage on the front line, followed by an advance still under heavy fire. Somewhere in the chaos of the next 24 hours Richard Hoskings lost his life.

The 21st Northumberland Fusiliers war diary for those three days shows that 7 officers and 21 other ranks were killed, and 5 officers and 147 other ranks wounded.

Richard's place of burial is unknown. He was 'Presumed Dead', and his death is commemorated on the Arras Memorial. He was posthumously awarded the British War and Victory Medals. The Arras memorial names 218 Northumberland Fusiliers killed in action on 5 June – none of whom has an identifiable grave.

My thanks to Michael D Strong and Shaun Flanagan

Edwin and (sitting) Richard Hoskings

Lilian Mosley's story

Much of this story comes from Annette Gunther, widow of Lilian's grandson Gerald and herself a farmer in New Zealand; my sincere thanks to her.

Lilian was Robert and Martha's second daughter and was born late in 1868. She seems to have had the privileged early life of the daughter of 'new landed gentry'. In the second half of 1899 she married Friedrich Carl Gunther – it is not at all clear how she met him. He was a man of mixed parentage, being born to a European and his concubine in Shanghai. His father was Danish, from Altona – in Schleswig-Holstein, a place which was ceded in about 1870 to Germany. Therefore once in England Friedrich was most commonly known as 'the German'. In those days companies apparently often supplied their European (and always male) staff with a 'concubine', whose name is generally unknown! Friedrich, later always known as Charles, and his sisters were educated in England, and he took two degrees (BA and BSc) and part of a medical degree before getting married.

Charles and Lilian settled in or near London – Stamford Hill in 1901 and the Chingford area in 1911. The 1911 census tells us that Charles was 41 and born in Shanghai; he was a schoolmaster. The couple had three children – John (9), Richard (6) and Ida (4 months). Charles taught at Epsom College (where he is still remembered) and the Hackney Grocers School. In 1947 he became a naturalised Briton, and members of both the Mosley and Hobson families sponsored his application. Charles died in Hove on 21 May 1948, and probate was granted to his widow Lilian. He left £228 14s 7d. Lilian died only months later, on 19 Apr 1949 and her estate came to £2,780 7s 5d.

Charles and Lilian had three children: Richard, John and Ida.

Richard, born in 1904 and known as Dick, settled in New Zealand where he married Mona M Munro in 1928. They had two children, Gerald, born in 1936, and Judith (born 1939). Gerald married Annette, the source of much of this information.

John was born in 1901 and married Alice Smelt, but had no children.

Ida was born in November 1910. On 2 Sept 1939 she married Victor Alexander Wilson Graham at Chelsea Old Church. They eventually moved to Australia, and Ida died in Adelaide in 1993.

In 1924 Dick was sent to New Zealand – he was only 20. There is a background story here of a misdemeanour on Richard's part which led to him being 'sent abroad'. It may have involved gambling, but details are unclear. John went with him - a late, hand-written, addition to the passenger list. Both left Liverpool on the Rimutaka and travelled third class, and both declared that they were farm workers, would land at Wellington, and in future reside in New Zealand.

However, it seems that neither was used to the 'working life' and they lived high with the polo set and ran through their money! Dick eventually settled down, became a dairy farmer and married Mona, but in 1933 John returned to England.

While both sons were still in New Zealand their mother Lilian and sister Ida made at least one visit – it was a long journey. They left England on 1 Oct 1930, on Hobsons Bay, and returned again in May 1931 on the same ship – travelling third class in both directions. They gave their address as 81 Stamford Hill, London N16. The family story of the visit is that Lilian expected to be waited on hand and foot, even though she was in New Zealand and even though she was a visitor – and that this was also later true of Ida!

Dick's son Gerald became a top-notch dairy farmer, and a breeder (and judge) of fine Jersey cattle.

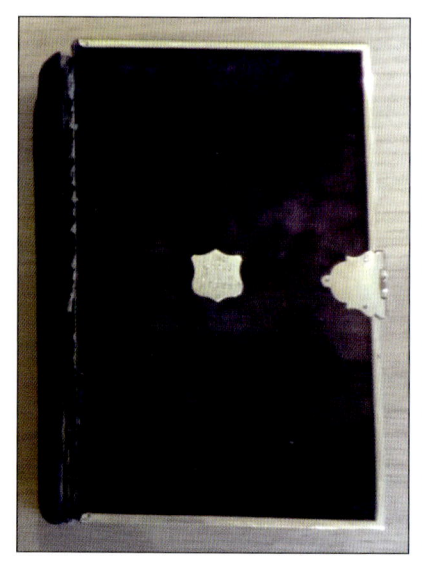

Annette has given Portland Works the small 'Family Bible' which had been passed down through the family, together with their hymnbook. Inscriptions in the Bible record the family story. They show M A Hobson (Martha), with a date that is probably her 21st birthday and then R F Mosley, with their wedding date. Lilian Mosley gave her 21st birthday; her daughter Ida Gunther recorded her birth date, and her son Gerald dated the book in 1997.

The Mosley family Bible

Albert Oswald Mosley

Albert was more commonly known as Bert and was married twice, first in 1903 to Florence May Brotherton, daughter of John and Louisa Brotherton of Stockton-on-Tees.

Bert was much younger than his brothers and had a bit of a history. It was almost certainly not expected that he would have to take over the company so soon after his father's death and he seems to have been allowed a fair bit of 'latitude' when he was young. However it came about, he ended up as the defendant in court in July 1907.

Only four years after his marriage to Florence he had an affair in Blackpool which resulted in him being sued for breach of promise. The young lady in question said he had asked her to marry him. The case was reported in great detail (left) in the Hull *Daily Mail* on 16 & 17 July 1907. Bert won his case but both parties came out of it very badly, the young lady being summed up as 'leading an immoral life' and the behaviour of Albert said to be 'as disgraceful as it is ever possible to hear of'. A shorter newspaper report of the case, source unknown, entitled 'Artist model's claim' sums it up well:

> **A LIGHTNING "COURTSHIP."**
>
> **"FAST" LIFE AT THE SEASIDE.**
>
> An action for breach of promise was heard at the Leeds Assizes on Monday, before Mr Justice Grantham. The plaintiff was Amy Berry, 41, Sheaf-gardens, Sheffield, and the defendant was Albert Oswald Mosley, of Messrs R. F. Mosley and Co., Ltd., Portland Works, Sheffield.

'The parties casually met in Blackpool, and for plaintiff it was stated an acquaintance sprung up, and marriage was promised. It was subsequently discovered that the defendant was a married man, and had adopted an assumed name. The defence was a denial of plaintiff's story. He was married in 1903, and had told his wife the whole story. He thought it was quite customary to meet a lady as he did and have a drive with her. He admitted they had a champagne dinner at Blackpool. The jury found a verdict for the defendant.'

It seems that, probably as a result of this case, Florence and Bert's young child (Robert Clive, known as Clive) was brought up for some of the time by his grand-parents RFM and Martha. This was quite possibly for his own safekeeping while his parents sorted out themselves and their relationship.

Psalter Lane

For all their married life Bert and Florence May lived on Psalter Lane. They were probably among the first people to live in the houses, which seem to have been built around 1900-1905.

At that time the houses were in a new area, being built along the road (formerly a salt route) leading from the new Abbeydale area out of town. These houses were apparently among the first developed, and built in fields. The house is in the middle of a high-quality terrace built on something of a ridge overlooking Sharrow Vale - and originally named, on a carved plaque, 'Psalter Terrace'. It is on four floors, only three of them visible from the road, owing to the sloping ground.

The lowest floor (or basement) was originally the kitchen area, though the only access to the garden was also through there. The floor included a kitchen, scullery, pantry and coal house (the latter two at the front of the house) as well as a toilet, presumably for the use of servants and gardeners.

The ground floor would have included the main drawing room, a dining room, and another room which may have been a breakfast room, or a servery of some sort for it includes access to the basement. All open off the hall, which leads via a staircase (with beautiful curved banister rail) to the upper floors.

The first floor is also 'main quarters' and has the main bedroom, the largest, towards the front of the house as well as a bathroom (originally divided into bathroom and toilet), a nursery and a further bedroom.

From there the stairs continue up to the second, or top, floor – which is smaller, as it is contained within the roof space and has sloping ceilings and dormer-style windows. These rooms would almost certainly have been 'servants quarters' – housing the housekeeper and / or maidservant.

Florence May died in June 1932 and was buried in the Mosley family vault at Fulwood; she left an estate of £6,525 12s 10d which was to be administered by her husband Bert and her son, both described as manufacturers. During the 1930s, as well, Portland Works was refinanced and restructured – and Bert and his new wife Marjorie moved further out of town to Fulwood Road.

Bert's house on Psalter Lane: outside, and in the hallway

By 1926 both Bert's older brothers, who had been key to both the firm and the relationship with Alexander Clark, were no longer working and Bert was running Portland Works. Because of economic conditions it was probably not a good time. Despite having a good start over other companies in the production of Rusnorstain (later more widely known as stainless steel) Bert must have been badly affected by the recession of the late 1920s.

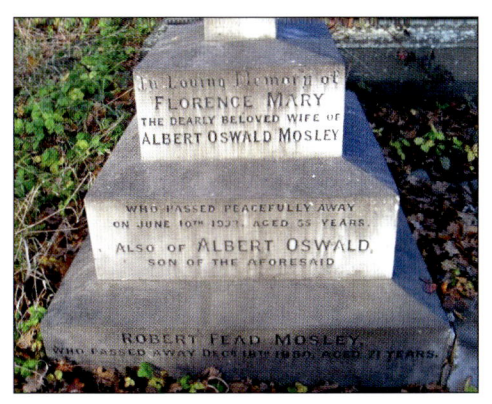

Florence died on 10 June 1932. She was buried in the Mosley grave (left). Bert remarried within three months – which usually counted as 'with indecent haste' in those days. However, things are not as dark as they might seem. We know that Bert had been unwell all his life, and that a relative on his mother's side had recently also been widowed. Apparently they married in order to be able to care for each other. His new wife was (Emily) Marjorie Richards but she was born with the surname Maxfield. She was the daughter of Ernest and Emily H Maxfield and a grand-daughter of Henry Hobson on her mother's side; she was always known to the family as Marjorie. Her father had been an electroplate manufacturer - almost certainly working with the Mosleys – but he died in 1902, aged 41.

In 1920 Marjorie had married Percy W Richards in Reading, but Percy died in 1924, aged only 43. A sad life, to have lost both a father and a husband so young. After she married Bert in 1932, Marjorie lived until 1948, but it is not clear where she was buried. We do have a snapshot of their life at 305 Fulwood Road in the census of 1939, and it serves to show how complex these two families were.

Living in the house that night, as well as Bert and Marjorie, were Marjorie's mother Emily Maxfield; two daughters - Marjorie's daughter by her first marriage, called Joan and now in her teens, and a joint child Marjorie Fay (always known as Fay); Harry A Ramsey, the American Vice Consul - who was married but whose wife was not with him; and three servants: Dorothy Haston, Jane Ann Reynolds and Lilian Holden.

Bert's life was complicated by his poor health, but his son joined the company as well. The *Sheffield Daily Telegraph* reported on 3 Feb 1930 that Robert Clive Mosley had been elected a director, and that he was a grandson of RFM, founder of the firm 70 years ago, and a son of Albert Oswald Mosley, the present chairman of the company.

Bert died on 18 December 1950 at the age of 71 and is buried in the Mosley vault. His estate came to £5,116 1s 8d. None of the three sons left an estate even approaching the size of RFM's; maybe the company depended on his personal energy and genius; or maybe, as with so many Sheffield cutlery makers, its heyday had passed.

Portland Works about the late 1960s, little changed.

R F Mosley & Co after 1921

The business continued after R F Mosley's death for around 50 years, and was run by his descendants – after his son Henry came Bert, who lived until 1950. The company was then taken over by his son Robert Clive Mosley, always known as Clive. He had married Winifred Audrey Savage in the second half of 1936. She was the daughter of Francis William and Jennie Savage, and was born in 1909 in Whittington Hill, Chesterfield; this is close to Harry Brearley's address. They had a son, John R Mosley, born in 1942, who ran the company from the time of his father's death until its closure in 1968.

Throughout these years there were trade difficulties, not the least of them being the Great Depression, the growth of mechanisation, and WW2. Stainless steel was also being produced by several cutlery companies. Manufacturers of costly luxury goods, such as silverware and even electroplate, were particularly vulnerable, maybe partly because stainless steel was cheaper, easier to clean and similar in appearance!

In the 1930s R.F. Mosley's went bankrupt and sold off its stock, prior to voluntary liquidation, although the company apparently then found enough money to carry on for it was reorganised and recapitalised under the old name.[26]

Information about this period is harder to discover, but here are a few stories about Portland Works.

The effects of mechanisation

An article in 1938 shows the effect on skilled workers of the increasing industrialisation of the cutlery processes. Arthur Redfearn, a successful grinder and recorder of the cutler's dialect, was forced to give up his cutlery life and become a dairyman. He had been a grinder, taught by his father, since he was 11 and had worked for firms including R F Mosley's. He became a member (and president for two years) of the Cutlery Trades Technical Society, and was also on the Cutlery Trades Board. But the introduction of machinery, and the girls who were able to manage the machines, left nothing for the skilled tradesman. 'The day is coming, and coming quickly, when trade will have to turn away orders because there will not be the men here to execute them'.[27]

A large fire in 1939

There was a major problem in the John Street / Randall Street area on the night of 5 Jan 1939. A newspaper report in the Sheffield Telegraph details the fire of the previous night. It was a freezing cold night with snow and ice on the pavements. A patrolling policeman saw flames, and tracked the fire down. Its heart was in the rear range of Portland Works, possibly in the second or third storeys.

Four fire engines quickly responded to the call but most of the rear range was well alight and they had to fight the flames from the top of escape ladders and from neighbouring rooftops. An added complication was that oils and lubricants were stored close to the Works, in the neighbouring premises of Wheen's - an Oil and Grease Works (now

Visible evidence of the 1939 fire

demolished) next to Stag Works on John Street. There was a danger that they might explode in the heat. John Street was closed and people were told to stay well away. Water from the hoses froze on the cobbled roads and added to the problems as flames poured out of the windows and through the roof.

In the end the fire was contained, but the top two storeys were badly damaged, along with the considerable amount of machinery contained in them. Reports say that seventeen cutlery workshops were destroyed, and 200 people put out of work because of the damage.

While the first floor was re-roofed the centre of the second was never rebuilt. So the external walls at each end of the flat roof were built as internal ones, with bricks of a lesser quality which were already fire-damaged. The forge was also rebuilt, with a flat roof rather than pitched. You can still see evidence of the effects of the fire, and many traces were found while the building was being repaired and re-decorated in 2018 – such as charring in the picture on the previous page. In addition the remaining top-floor roofs of Block C seemed hardly to be attached to the walls anymore! There was still a great deal of charring in roof-beams and window-frames. Remedying it involved a lot of unforeseen work.

The fire cannot have helped, as the company struggled soon afterwards with the effects of war. Many of the workers had to move to munitions work in the steel factories, and so there was a reliance on younger people, many without the skills of former employees.

Because of the threat of air raids the chimney was reduced to half its height, in common with many unused but stately chimneys in Sheffield, and the basement area (see page 30) was bricked up and transformed from silver-smithing into an air raid shelter.

The Blitz

The Sheffield Blitz, the main attacks being over two nights in December 1940, hit several areas of Sheffield very badly, and also extended out to the Highfield area. It is not clear whether Mosley's ever suffered a direct bombing hit, but the Works was certainly affected by incendiaries, probably on the night of 15 December 1940.

The pencil-written letter below is on R F Mosley headed paper, and was sent to us by Annette Gunther, Gerald's widow. It was written to Gerald when he was about 4, by his grandmother Lilian, R F Mosley's daughter. Although it is undated, we know that bombs fell in this area during the Sheffield blitz on 15 December 1940.

My darling Gerald

You will like to have this picture of your Great Grandfathers works which were built by him in 1880 and is still in the Mosley family, and you are named after them. Give Judith our love. Grandad is so pleased with your letter, & thinks you write quite well. I will send you a bigger picture one day & you must always keep it.

Your Great Grandfather was the first to make Stainless Knives. Well I am at the works with your Great-Uncle Bertie. Must end as Grandad has just arrived to look over the works. Some bombs (fire ones) fell on it, but they got the fires out.

Love to you & darling Judith Anne. Also Mummie and Daddy.

Your ever loving Granny.

The later history of the Works

After Bert's death in 1950 the directors included his son and the company was exporting much of its output to Australia. However, former British colonies were gaining their freedom and setting up their own industrial centres. It was something of a disaster when Mosley's was faced with losing four-fifths of its Australia trade in 1952, as is revealed by a letter published in *The Sydney Morning Herald* on 20 March. It contains a quote from Clive Mosley, Bert's son and managing director of Mosley's: 'The Australian imports ban has come as a great shock to us all at the factory, as we have £10,000 worth of goods in our packing-room awaiting permit, which, it seems, will fill our quota for the whole year. We are very down-hearted at the moment about this, as it will be a catastrophe to discharge most of our workpeople.'

The writer goes on to add that 'It is a tragedy to think that the present restrictions are likely to react so drastically on the activities of such an old-established organisation and to bring about what might be loss of employment to artisans who have spent a lifetime in developing their skill.'

> **Handles!**
> In Ernest Stuart's time Mr Senior was the handle-maker. He made handles in all materials, and other cutlers would buy in from him.
>
> By the 1960s handles were made by Drakes on Bramall Lane, and delivered to the Works.

Sure enough, R F Mosley's did struggle, and laid off workers soon afterwards. It continued to trade, sharing more of the works with other businesses and with fewer actual employees, but the writing was on the wall and the end finally came in the late 1960s.

Papers given to us following the death of Pam Stuart, Ernest's grand-daughter, tell the story. During the 1960s the company kept going, paying a dividend to shareholders and maintaining a small profit to re-invest. However, by 1965 this was no longer tenable, and a lengthy note in the Annual Report for 1966 tells us that 'due to adverse trading conditions and the inability to replace work-people who had left the Company's employment, it was not possible to carry on the trading of the Company efficiently.

The directors came to the conclusion, very reluctantly after the many years the Company had been trading as cutlery manufacturers, that they had no alternative but to cease the manufacture of goods. This step was taken on 29 October 1965, the majority of the stock and the trade mark being taken over by another firm in the cutlery trade. The turning point for the company was a government contract for the supply of knives which they were unable to fulfil, and consequently had to pay an excess for an alternative supplier to be found. The payment turned a small profit into a loss. The company was closed, but Mosley's retained the premises and its machinery, which were already let to various tenants.

The next year, the annual meeting was held on 20 March 1967. There was another long note in the accounts reporting that efforts were in hand to sell Portland Works to a new owner, if one could be found. By August that year a purchaser had been found and the company reported that it was considered to be 'in the interests of the shareholders, bearing in mind the present taxation provisions affecting Companies, if the Company was wound up'. The company directors at the time were all family members – Robert Clive Mosley (Bert's son, always known as Clive), John R Mosley (Clive's son) and Winifred Audrey Mosley (Clive's wife) but the number and identity of shareholders is not known.

The Sipelia Group, a flatware company, took over the company name and trademark. It had been founded in the 1930s by a German man named Sippel. However, it too went bankrupt in 1972 and 'R F Mosley' was liquidated for the last time.[28]

Harry Marriott – Portland Works' own ghost
Told by Colin Jessop, more-or-less in his own words.

The Works was supposed to have been haunted. The rumour was that the ghost was an old bloke who used to be caretaker here.

One of the metal-smiths did a runner one night, he got frightened by something. He was working over at his bench and the door from the corridor opened. It was on a spring, and just opened on its own, and a man came in and walked across the floor. Then the man went through another door, and the metal-smith spoke to him but he just ignored him. Two minutes later the man came back and just walked past him again and he said 'Are you alright?' - again he just ignored him.

About five seconds later Tony Wardle (the boss) walked in, so this metal-smith said 'Who were that?' Tony said 'Who were who?' He said 'Who were that bloke? You must have passed him on the stairs.' Tony said 'Nobody's passed me on the stairs'. So he described him to him – black cap, white stock round his neck. And Tony says 'Oh, it's Harry. Harry Marriott. He used to be caretaker here but when they retired him he didn't want to retire. So he hanged himself.' The bloke picked all his stuff up, and said to Tony 'I'm not coming here again, mate.'

A few years later Colin was working for Bob Leary's pewter, in the same place. One day Bob said: 'I've got to work all night, do you mind coming in and working with me all night?' I said 'No chance, I'm going out.' He said 'Come on, I'll pay you extra.' Again I said 'No, I'm going out. But I'll come back about four o'clock.' When I came back at 4 o'clock I walked through the arches and there were oil drums and sacks and pieces of wood all over the stairs because he was frightened. I said 'But if it's a ghost it can walk through them!'

Sometimes we'd work till nine, ten o'clock at night. One thing that did happen to us, we were sat there having snap – our tea – because we were working till late that night. And in the lantern room we heard a clinking: like a crate of tankards and one was catching the other tankards and making a noise.

So the four of us went through, and there was a tankard spinning on the floor. Now we thought it was somebody messing about so we split up and went different ways and into the end shop – nobody there. It was a bit scary. I thought it was just somebody messing about but there was nobody. And we came back here and the tankard was still on the floor, it had stopped spinning.

We thought it was someone joking with us. But when that tankard came out and started spinning round on the floor, it did make me think. The number of times I worked here - and I was on my own at night!

Who was Harry Marriott?

Harry's full name was Walter Harry Marriott, and he was born in 1891, to a father with exactly the same name. By 1912, just married, he and his wife Hilda lived in Portland Works, by the entrance. As maintenance engineer he took care of the gas engines and dealt with any problems. He certainly lived there until the 1948 street directory was published, but had gone before the 1951 edition; after that, his house became part of the Works. That was about the time when Bert Mosley died, and things probably changed as a result. Harry moved a little nearer London Road but maybe never got used to a new life. He died on 3 January 1959 at the Royal Hospital. He seems to have hanged himself back at 'his' works, where he had lived for over thirty years.

Annie Warburton

Annie Warburton was nearly 90 when we interviewed her, but she remembered starting work at Mosley's, where her grandmother worked, in about 1938. What is below is some of the story as she told it.

Annie was 14 when she started work at Portland Works, working in the buffing shop at the end of the Hill Street range. By this time Mosley's was run by just one or two people, who gave work to other independent (or self-employed) people working closely with them in the yard. Annie used to work for Ernest Lashley running errands, but she also had certain routines and jobs to do. First thing in the morning she used to sweep the workshops. Next she would go to Laycocks to fetch any buffs, rouge and so on that were needed for the buffing shop. After that it was water-carrying: bringing zinc buckets up from the only drinking water tap at the back of the yard and up two floors of stone steps to the buffing shop. The bucket would go on the fire to get hot for pots of tea.

Monday was 'Buffers Monday', and the buffers would finish at half past eleven, as soon as the pub was open, and go down to the pub at The Sportsman, facing the football ground. Her grandmother had her own chair there, that no-one else dared to sit in. The buffers all left their coats and baskets at the Works – but actually never came back for them, so Annie would carry a great heap of coats, bags and baskets down to the pub. She wasn't allowed in because of her age, so when they saw her arrive someone would have to come out of the pub to carry it all in.

She would bring dinners from local shops. They used to say 'Come and fetch us some sandwiches from Taylors on London Road' so she'd go up there first, take them what they wanted, then to the pie shop, the chip shop. And if she was late there was trouble! After that she would go back and mash teas, then go back down, get some water for their hands and carry it all the way up again. It was about half a dozen times a day she carted buckets up and down so the buffer girls could wash their hands at dinner time and when they went home.

Everything that was done for Mosley's had to be 'A1' – their standards were very high. After finishing buffing and polishing they would go down to Mosley's warehouse with trays of what they had done. Annie told a story that once she finished a ladle and a big fork for them – it had to be done properly, and she knew that it was good work. However, the story of why she had done it got twisted by another woman, and shortly afterwards Annie left Portland Works.

Bert Housley

Bert Housley worked at Portland Works for his father's firm, which was in the back range. His father had three workshops – a grinding wheel, a place for doing the cutlery-glazing, and an office. In 1939 the corner of the ground floor of his part of the works was surrounded by sandbags and it became a further air-raid shelter.

Bert was also a master photographer, and we are grateful for his help with the 1908 photographs, many of which sharpened up. He was also able to explain them for us as he knew the old cutlery terminology.

The blades were forged in the goff shop – the process was known as goffing. Forging table knives by hand was done on a tree-trunk. They said that there was horse manure underneath it, to make it more resilient. The smiths were known as 'hotters and colders' because they heated up the blades and then cooled them down again.

Then there was grinding, a filthy job. It is apparent from records of the time that grinders had a very low life expectancy because of the fine dust which got into their lungs. Many died before they were forty.

In the grinding wheel the only form of lighting was gas, and in the photo on the next page you can see gas pipes running to where the grinders are working, and where men are doing glazing along the back.

One of the grinding shops, probably on the first floor.

There were wide leather belts taking the power from big gas engines (see one below) to workshops on the first and second floors. If all the grinders were working hard the load could slow the engine down, and the noise could be horrendous.

'One stone burst in John Street while I was in the navy during the war and one of the buffer girls, who actually worked for my Dad, had the habit of going in the teabreak and standing in front of the fire in the grinding wheel. When this stone burst half of it hit her and killed her outright; the grinder was thrown in the air and landed on the boards at the back of the grinding wheel.'

In the buffing shop there were many different sized buffs, hundreds of them. If you were doing a coffee spoon you used a tiny buff with the sand to get inside the bowl; for big silverware bowls you had much bigger buffs.

The double-heading machine was a machine with two buffs, but Mosley's did not know how to use one properly. You had two treadles – when you put the blade in you could raise and lower it with the left-hand pedal to cover every part of the blade; the right-hand pedal brought the wheels together so you could get a lot of pressure. But to dress them was a terrible job. 'Arrogant as I was I went to Mosley's and I knew they weren't using the double-heading machines. I said if you'll let me come in and work on them, you needn't pay me if they're not good enough. Anyway they set me on and I was only working about six hours a day but and I was earning more than I was before!'

The first floor (of D block) was mostly rented out to self-employed cutlers. One was Mr Turner, an elderly man who was an ivory-carver. His speciality was making tea-knives in sets of twelve, all slightly different.

The gas engine only ran during the day. Harry Marriott was the engine tender, and he was quite fierce. His ears were tuned to the engines, and wherever he was in the factory if any sound came through that was strange he would be dashing down the yard. When you were working there, 'You didn't hear anything unless it was a sound that shouldn't have been there, and then you heard it!'

In the workshop right opposite the archway in 1939 was a man who gathered used toothpaste tubes and removed the tops. Then he melted the tubes down so they could be re-used, and earned a good living doing that.

Occupants of Portland Works

This is the story of firms working at Portland Works, according to directories (Kelly's, White's etc) in Sheffield Local Studies Library. It takes no account of the 'oral history' stories collected.

Until about the time of the Second World War the Hill Street range (with one exception) was apparently only accessed through the archway – the doorway to the street at the far end of the range was an addition.

The exception was the house (to the left of the archway) that was occupied by the caretaker / maintenance engineer. From 1889 this house was lived in by Joseph and Eliza Pearson: Eliza is described as a dressmaker. Joseph was still caretaker in 1898, but then Eliza took on the role until 1904. Her place was taken from 1905 to 1910 by Frost Ellis, engineer, who was in turn replaced by Walter Harry Marriott (jnr), also an engineer. He continued in post until about 1950, when 79 Hill Street became part of E Atkinson & Sons premises.

In the late 1930s two addresses were added to Hill Street, for a new door was inserted at the far end of the Works which led to nos 71 and 73. It made this range, and some of that side of the works, accessible without going through the Works gate, and therefore easier to let. It is possible that the change was prompted by the fire of 1939, though it may pre-date the blaze.

Both addresses, often also including no 79, were occupied by two companies, on different floors. From 1948 to 1958 these were William Needham (cutlery manufacturer) and E Atkinson and Sons (makers of painters' tools). In 1958 Brown Bros Ltd (motor tyre factors and distributors) moved in as well, and William G Ridgway is an additional tenant at 79. By 1968 the numbering was quite complex (and probably fairly irrelevant to anyone but the postman) but this was the situation: at 71 was M Coombes, hunting knife manufacturer; 71/73 were occupied by William Needham; 71, 73 and 79 by E Atkinson and Brown Bros, and William Ridgway was also still in at least part of 79. This was largely the case until 1972, except that William Ridgway left around 1970.

The main yard of Portland Works was listed on Randall Street, for that is where both the archway and the main office street door are to be found. From the very beginning R F Mosley & Co (silversmiths and cutlery manufacturers) shared the works with J T Johnson & Sons, steam joinery manufacturers; my suspicion is that it was Johnson's who made the fine-quality cabinets for cutlery and silver which Mosley's used. From 1930 Mosley's no longer described themselves as silversmiths in directories, keeping the listing purely to cutlery manufacture.

In 1931 the listing was supplemented by Clark's (The Alexander Clark Cutlery Works) which for so many years had been in a symbiotic partnership between Clark and Mosley. The 1936 directory makes this clear, for Clark is named as a manufacturing silversmith and Mosley's as a cutlery manufacturer. In that same year they were joined in the yard by Moorhead Supplies Ltd, refrigerating engineers, who stayed until 1938 or so – at which point Alexander Clark also disappears from the listings, for he died and the link between the two families disappeared.

After January 1939 there must have been considerable changes, because of the big fire in Block C that month, but its effects are not seen at all in the directories.

All through the Second World War the only listing is for R F Mosley & Co – but whether this reflects the actual situation or a lack of money or energy for advertising by other tenants it is impossible to say. In 1948 Mosley's are joined by L Allen, silversmith and, just for one year in 1951, there is an explosion of listing. A dozen small workshops, all grinders, advertised their presence in the directory alongside Mosley and Allen: Charlesworth & Jones, Bernard Cocker, George Harry Wilson, Stanley Linley, Fred Ashton, George Allen, Leonard Whomersley, John William Roberts, Herbert Starr and Thomas Trownslaw & Son.

From 1954 the more usual listing is resumed, with RF Mosley's and L Allen's alone at first. They were joined in 1961 by W R Humphreys & Co Ltd, cutlery manufacturers, and J W Hampshire, stainless carver fork manufacturer. This expansion in the number of other tenants reflects Mosley's continuing decline and decrease in size. By 1963 J W Hampshire has gone, and O Hobson, general & precision engineers, moves into the works. In 1965 they were joined by Pass Sheet Metal, sheet metal workers.

1968 is the last directory to list R F Mosley, who went into liquidation. Occupants of the works that year were: R F Mosley & Co, cutlery manufacturers; O Hobson, general & precision engineers; Eadon Litho Ltd, lithographic offset machine plate makers; Fabricated Products, fabrication in steel; Swales & Coward, manufacturers of tyre pressure gauges; Wardle & Matthews Ltd, pewter ware manufacturers; and Pass Sheet Metal, sheet metal workers. The character of Portland Works was no longer a cutlery works, but a collection of manufacturing workshops.

The last days of Mosley's - Bob and Anne Slater

Bob and Anne Slater knew some of the Mosleys well: John Mosley is their son's godfather. Bob was a painter and decorator, and Anne was employed at the Works. They also remember his father Clive Mosley – a man 'nothing like a businessman' who was very tall and well-built. He was also very laid back: 'There was once a small fire at the factory, evening time, and the fire brigade came. We rang him up to say "You've got a fire at the factory." And he came down, and parked his car in the road, and there's his factory with a fire engine, and he turned round and he said "Ooh, look at that lovely sunset!"'

While Anne worked there Mosley's offices and packing-rooms were still upstairs. There were several other tenants too. Down at the far end of the yard was the buffing shop, and in the corner grinding shops with big grinding wheels – Frank Booth worked there. In the centre workshop was the forge Wigfull's, where a father and son worked. The power was switched on at 7am, and off again at 7pm – there was no working outside those hours.

The grinding shops were dangerous, the engines all-electric with a big belt on a drum. While you were concentrating on the grinding there was a great belt whipping round your legs! And bits were always burning down, for the dust off the handles was very flammable – so extractor fans were used where necessary. They made ceremonial topping-out trowels, because you need a new one every time.

In the Hill Street side, up the staircase, was Needham's; as he was a painter and decorator Bob used to get his blades there.

When Mosley's closed Bob helped John Mosley to strip it all out. They would take down all the line-shafts for the scrapman, and split the proceeds between them. Some of them were 300 feet long, and the value was about £10 a ton.

A few parts of line-shafts still remain; this pulley is one of them

As we renovate the Works, we discover more parts that still remain, which can help our understanding of the building. The post-boxes on the next page are still in the entrance archway and date from Mosley days. The boxes are still in use. At that time there was also a 'clocking-in machine' on the opposite wall.

From time to time we also discover small caches of interesting remains. Forty fragments of cutlery were all found in one place between the floors in Block D when a ceiling was renewed. It is where we believe that hafting had been done. Some of them have now been put in a display case. It clearly shows broken knives, and blades that were worn in curious ways. The blades had been used as tools to shape handles, and were then almost certainly shoved down a hole in the floor to conceal their mis-use. It was those we had found.

Portland Works - 1968 to 2010

Information about tenants of a particular building becomes harder to find in modern times, as the Kelly-type directory was no long produced. But these are some of the stories we have been told. To set the scene, we start with someone who grew up across the road in the 1960s.

The area – Mike Tomlinson

Before 1968 Mike lived with his parents at 78 Randall Street, opposite Portland Works. Portland Works still belonged to Mosley's. There was a brass plaque (polished most mornings) on the wall to the right of the main door, and wording all along the building. In the archway was the clocking-on machine, with the cards alongside it. Mike's next–door neighbour Les Holmes had a driving school, and had two cars. One was their own, old and with a running-board, and the other was a Ford Anglia which Mike drove to take his driving lessons.

The corner shop was Ellis's, a complete shop going back into the yard. 'I remember they had a big slab of cheese or of butter: you'd go in and they'd cut it, a little bit of it, and you'd take it back in a little bag.' Even in those days it seemed old. Behind it was a yard, shared between four houses, with the loos at the very back. On the opposite corner was Giles's – it was the 'beer-off' sort of shop. The houses up Randall Street had small gardens at the front with walls, but here over the crossroads they didn't.

Next to Portland Works was Fox and Robinson, a wood merchants with a big steel gate, then a bigger house where maybe the boss lived. Mike said that there was bomb damage along there, still unrepaired from the war.

The Cricketers, where Mike's father used to go, still exists at the end of the road.

And now to some of the resident tenants of Portland Works of the time.

E Atkinson & Sons Ltd, *with thanks to Gillian Johnson (nee Atkinson)*

This company was at Portland Works from before the end of WW2 until 1973. It was started by Edward Atkinson and continued by his two sons Albert (known as Mick) and Edward Jnr (Ted). They made painters' tools and other hand tools. The company workshops were listed as 71-73 Hill Street – accessed by a door created just before the war to allow easy entry to the Hill Street range.

In 1949 the company applied for a patent for an improved screwdriver, which was patented and launched in 1952 and known as 'Perfect' or 'Per-cab'. The patent covered the linking of the handle and blade in a way which made the tool much stronger and the handle less inclined to split.

Between 1963 and 1965 the firm expanded into 79 Hill Street (formerly the caretaker's cottage). This was to give sufficient space for new legal requirements of washing and eating facilities, including toilets and drinking water. Gillian said 'I can remember the discussions that went on at home about what a waste of money it was and how a bit of dirt had never hurt anyone. No doubt this echoed the thoughts of many owners of workplaces all over the country.'

Gillian used to help out at Hill Street. When she was about 8 her father Mick would take her round the outworkers to collect the tool-parts. This included the ground blanks and the handles, which were then put together in Hill Street. In her teens Gillian was given a holiday job. Each morning she made up a supply of packing boxes and then oiled blades prior to packing the tools in half-dozens or dozens.

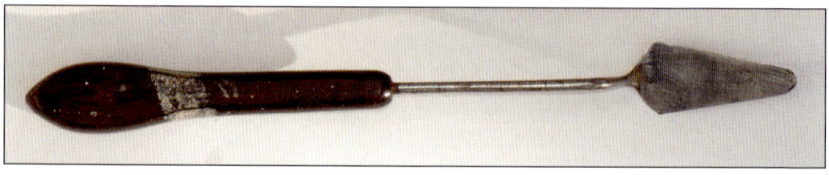

'My most vivid memory is of a time around the early 60s. The firm had a large order to supply small black handled screwdrivers to Woolworths, which was targeting the new craze for DIY ... Our marketing gimmick was sticking a small Union flag on the handle of each screwdriver emphasising the object had been Made in Britain. These came on rolls of Sellotape (like the robins at Christmas time) and I had to cut off each one and stick it on before packing the required number in the box.'

E Atkinson & Sons came to an end in 1972 with Mick's sudden death, aged only 61. His brother Ted was devastated and did not want to continue on his own. He agreed a merger with Hamilton's of Dronfield and the company closed and moved there. However, Ted's son Glyn continued to work for Hamilton's until he retired.

Emil and Ruby Berek, *with thanks to Don Alexander*

Berek was born in Poland, on the border with Czechoslovakia. He fought in WW2 for the Polish Army and the French Resistance, and arrived in England in 1947. He was just 21, and over the next 20 years built up a network of small companies – but keeping their English names and original identity. Berek thought this easier for trade. Two of these companies were in Portland Works: Berek bought the Needham business, and also traded as J Y Cowlishaw. John Yeomans Cowlishaw died in 1895 and as far as we are aware never himself traded from Portland Works, but his name was presumably later used by others.

Berek spent £400, a lot of money then, decorating the upper room. He also had a little runaround van. He kept both names, mostly because he was proud to continue the Sheffield tradition of craftsmanship; a further reason was suspicion of a foreign-looking name in the knife industry. In 1971 the *Sheffield Morning Telegraph* featured Emil (26 May). He saw that expansion would have been possible, but preferred a grinding wheel to a machine because of the quality obtainable. 'I am not interested in a posh office but I am interested in production. An efficient business with 25 people is more profitable than an inefficient business with 100.' Emil was 47 at the time, and regularly worked 50 hours a week – but also liked relaxation and 'good living'. Among other things Emil made 'Slim Jim' pocket knives with two blades for Wilkinson Sword and three-bladed pocket knives for the Ministry of Defence. Cowlishaw's employed around 20 people.

Emil's wife Ruby, a Sheffielder, was also in business at Portland Works, making jewellery with her manager Ray Wildsmith. During the 1970s there was a craze for items made with abalone shell. The business was known as Ruby Ray Jewellery and was an economical set-up, for she was able to use scrap and offcuts.

Emil and Don set up a stall on Rotherham market selling Sheffield goods. However, Emil and Ruby were two of four people who died in a car crash on the Ringinglow Road on 7 October 1974. The crash was reported in the newspapers the next day. Emil was known as a fast driver, but their deaths were a great shock. Ray continued to run the jewellery business for a while, but then the whole concern was sold. After Ray died, his wife continued making wire baskets for a while.

Don said that sorting out the business was a bit of a nightmare, for there was very little proper paperwork. There were no receipts or anything for Emil's machinery, and company security could best be called non-existent. Emil apparently simply had rolls of money in his pocket, and silver and gold knives sitting on the table! 'It was a successful business, but chaotic.'

Rainbow Angling / Trakker *thanks to Jayne Binns, and the Drabble family at Trakker*

Trakker Products, who are still in business, began life as Rainbow Angling Supplies back in 1983. The company was started by Carl Drabble and set up in what is now the Makerspace area to the front of the Portland Works building. The company was created during the recession of the early 1980s when Sheffield's traditional industries of steel and cutlery were hit badly, as a result Carl found himself out of work.

Always a keen angler, Carl had always had the dream of making a career from his hobby and so set about making it reality by setting up a manufacturing facility producing luggage and clothing, at its peak employing up to 40 sewing machinists. Portland Works helped enormously in the difficult early years due to rent being very affordable which allowed overheads to be kept to a minimum; as the business grew Rainbow Angling took up an increasingly greater space in the building before eventually having to relocate to larger premises.

Jayne Binns was on a college placement with Rainbow Angling in about 1986. At that time the company made bags of various sorts and thermal suits, and she remembers working with about 10 people in the sewing factory. It could be cold in winter, so they 'double-glazed' the many windows with polythene and had a portable gas heater.

At the time the large space was subdivided into two or three spaces – a little office, a small area with cups and a kettle, and a large room which had machines by the front windows and a large cutting table behind. Jayne was only there for a year, and remembers the scooters over the road in Armando's (still there!). And one day 'we were sitting there at lunchtime and a cricket ball came crashing through the window. We looked through and all the men were rushing away like naughty children!'

Trakker survives to this day and now has premises just off the Sheffield Parkway as well as a large facility in Slovakia servicing the European market; none of this would have been possible without Portland Works.

Wardle & Matthews (pewter)

Colin Jessop was the son of Mary, who was a spoon and fork buffer who worked, mostly in Block C, for various companies. Her work included a lot of 'out work' for firms such as Roberts & Belk. Colin came to work with pewter manufacturers on the top floor of the Randall Street range.

During the 1960s Wardle and Matthews had all the top floor in the front of the Works. To the left of the stairs were offices and a small workshop. On the other side were metal-smiths all along, with a buffing shop on the other side; one of the buffing rooms had the luxury of a toilet built in one corner! There was a little curved casting shop (for making handles) over the archway. About 20 people worked for them.

On leaving the Works Wardle and Matthews moved to Attercliffe, but closed around 2003. After they left, the space was taken by Bob Leary, who

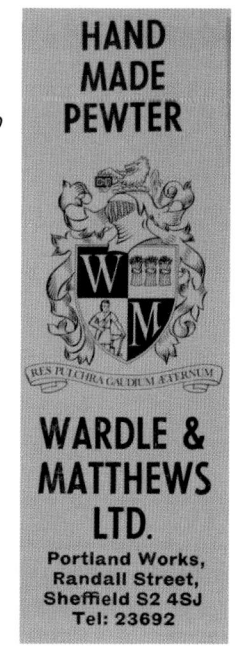

HAND MADE PEWTER

WARDLE & MATTHEWS LTD.

Portland Works,
Randall Street,
Sheffield S2 4SJ
Tel: 23692

also had part of his works further on through the buffing shop, in the upper floor of Block G. He did a lot of work for Viners but manufactured pewter tankards himself.

William Needham

William Needham's was founded in the late 19th century, and moved to Portland Works just after WW2. Maybe they took advantage of the new access to workshops on Hill Street because of the addition of a roadside outside door. As well as part of Portland Works they also occupied, and had their sign over, the whole of the building next door. This building still exists, but has been converted to be part of Go Outdoors on Hill Street. Needhams made and sold cutlery, not only for the table but also for other purposes (such as sportsmen's knives). It was still at the Works in the early 1970s.

W Beal

W Beal made scissors at Portland Works – continuing a tradition begun by Robert Mosley. His range included surgical scissors and also palette knives for the kitchen and knives for butchers. Little else is known about him, but he appears in street directories.

Betts Tools

The early story of Betts Tools is at the Works, though the company was still in Sheffield until recently. Both Andy Cole and Stuart Mitchell remember them. They occupied a large amount of the Works, including a bit of the rear ground floor which had previously held grinding machines. It still had a couple of surface grinders but now contained a garden shed as their office! Stuart remembers they had a heat treatment place, where he could go 'while the lads were having their sandwiches – I could go in and do our hardening and tempering'. Stuart's sisters worked for Stan Betts upstairs at the front of the Works, where there was a screen printing workshop. Betts Tools eventually moved on to Carlisle Street, and set up Betts R&D where research on levels was done.

Accounts told by Andy Cole

Bill Turner

Bill Turner had one of the old grinding machines. Like all of them 'it had a big barrel at the back that was the drive, and then it went down to the shaft, then ran the shafts; but I always remember the one he always worked on, the bearings was a V-block of wood with a lump of lard stuck on top. There were literally no health and safety, and I once commented about a piece of wood strapped to his leg. He said "Don't you know what that is?" and afterwards it was obvious, it was his emergency stop. Because the belt would run past him, the big flat belt, and he just shoved the belt off with his leg, and that was his emergency stop.'

Pass Steel (Ted Jenner)

When Andy Cole started work the middle of the rear range was still a grinding shop. There was a little step all along there and a lorry used to reverse in and drop plate steel on the floor - all of it cut into sizes 4x9, 5x9 and 7x9 inch. They were razor sharp but had to be sorted out. Andy used to pick them up, sort them and stack them. The office for Pass Steel was at the front of the Works, later occupied by Paul Hopprich, and their sign is still on steps in the small yard.

Pete and Alan

Pete and Alan worked next door to Bill Turner. Right at the front was a large press, with three snow (or surface) grinders behind - one was a little one that used to put the bevel on a wood chisel. And next to the grinders was a hardening tank. Pete was always known as 'Lippy Pete' (not thought right these days!) but it was because of his hare lip.

Musicians

For many years Portland Works has been home to a variety of musicians and bands. Its situation means that practising does not disturb the neighbours, for it is part of a non-residential block. Moreover, the dilapidated condition has meant that bands felt able to take steps to soundproof it and to reduce echoes for recording. We have also been able to draw on the expertise of some of the bands who currently rehearse in the Works to help with sound amplification at our events.

Two of the bands who have rehearsed here in the past are Def Leppard, pictured (below) a number of years ago on the roof of C Block, and in more recent years The Gentlemen.

Saving Portland Works

Thanks to Derek Morton and Julia Udall

A Beginning: Speculation (in 2009)
Julia Udall, Senior Lecturer in Architecture, Sheffield Hallam University

Beginnings are often hard to pin down; where does a story start, and for whom? What are the layers of work that have gone before to make something possible? Why do some moments that might be a closing down, an end, instead become an opening of possibility?

I first encountered Portland Works, as a student, relatively new to the city of Sheffield. It was a beautiful, though (even to my well-disposed eyes) bedraggled, curved brick building, close to Bramall Lane football ground. I was there as part of an architecture student project with Sheffield University.

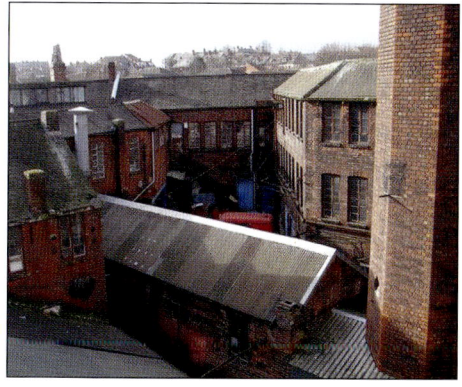

Our brief, offered by Sharrow Community Forum Director Colin Havard, was to think about how this dense and rapidly changing area of factories, car lots, shops and light industry might offer skilled employment for the neighbourhood of Sharrow - and what the role the physical environment might have in this. The student whose designated bit of the map included Portland Works returned to the University Arts Tower studio, thrilled with his encounter - the people, the skills, the architecture; his photographs glowed with colour and material and stuff. We wove them in to proposals to activate courtyards, make more use of the streets, support community facilities, metalwork, arts and food markets. The Forum's enthusiasm for our resultant student project led to me being employed as a Community Architectural Researcher, and in the months that followed, working to develop the Distinctive Sharrow Masterplan.

Funding for such a community role at the time was the result of hard work to articulate its potential value. Now the possibility of a community organisation supporting such work in the UK seems difficult to imagine.

One of the first calls I received at my new desk at the Forum was from Frances Cole of Wigfull Tools, to tell me that Portland Works was under threat. She said that their landlord had turned up and told them that he was turning the Works into flats - and because it was a Change of Use he had the right to evict all the tenants. It did not matter how long-standing their tenancies, or how thriving their businesses. She told me how this felt. She told me that for many it would be the end of their business. This call wasn't to be her last, and we became friends. Many a day she rang, telling me stories of the Works - family Christmases where work still had to be done and snowmen were built by their children in the Works courtyard, histories of manufacturing and Mesters, who was there and what they did, the weekly results of her persistent work in Sheffield Archives digging up photographs, fragments of people's lives, all building up a rich picture of why this place mattered - to her, to those who had businesses here, to the city.

These stories were of hard work, under difficult conditions. They were of friendships, frustrations, women, men, children. Of metal, of tools, of machinery. Of certain ways of being together. Sure of the need to be there to really understand, Frances invited me to visit the Works during the Galvanise Festival - to see demonstrations of work, to meet tenants, to hear of their fight against the planning application. What came across was this was a certain way of doing-together in the city. I wanted to take a part in the struggle to save Portland Works, and felt this wasn't just about one approach, or one set of people, it was a place that was connected to arts and manufacturing and culture across many decades. It wasn't just about how much money these businesses contributed to the local economy, or Sheffield's marketed image as 'steel city'.

It was a fight against gentrification, and also a collective thinking into the future of the city. It was about the sitting side-by-side of artists, musicians and metalworkers, and precarious livelihoods supported by friendships, mutualism, skill and care. It was about the kinds of space that we had in Sheffield, and what could happen in them.

As an architect I worked to analyse the Planning Application and understand points of leverage, legitimate objections, statutory possibilities. As a student I called on lecturers at Sheffield University with understanding of social and cultural movements and design-based action. As a part of the Forum I could raise the issue politically, bringing in the local Labour and Green councillor and city planners. I could also go out to the streets and tell people about it; local residents, businesses; community and cultural organisations. As part of Social Enterprise Architectural Practice Studio Polpo I could enthuse those in our practice to offer their design expertise to Portland Works. As an Architectural Design Tutor I could invite students to speculate on what might happen next, and to compile careful surveys of the area as evidence to support our fight against planning permission. I also told friends; artists, musicians, designers, activists in the city… anyone who might listen, and asked them how they might take part.

    Toolmaker Andrew Cole had worked to get the Master Cutler and local MP involved. Artist-tenants had determined to squat. Visitors to the Galvanise Metalwork Festival had learnt about the situation from the Mesters who showed them around their studios and demonstrated their craftsmanship. Metalwork tenants knew they had a powerful narrative of their work, and the history of the Mesters. Councillors went door-to-door. Musicians and artists drew on networks to set up and host festivals and events.

    The Chair of the Forum had recently led a campaign to support the redevelopment of the adjacent Stag Works (now largely music studios, but still occupied by some metalworkers) and his surveys and feasibility work in the area was offered for our use. Pictures of Sheffield Old and New (then only a handful of members now over 37,000), drew together photographers to document the Works and convened an exhibition at Castle Market to support the campaign. Politicians from the Green Party and Labour featured us in campaign materials, and Bank Street Arts offered us gallery space to exhibit artefacts produced at Portland Works.

    Sometimes, to come together around an existential threat leads to an opening up, rather than a closing down. Such happenings are stories of infrastructures and of people. Capacities for collective and transformative actions are produced by building layers of networks, practices, values and support. This is social and political work emerging over many years.

    Portland Works became a place that convened a community around a concern. For those who responded to an emerging situation there must be a willingness to not know-for-sure, to find out with others, to speculate. This risk of 'keeping open' is not evenly distributed - many tenants' livelihoods were at risk - yet there was a passionate fight not only to save their businesses, but to push for this kind of space within the city, for the learning of others. In the work I did towards the project I tried to make multiple stories of the place, with possibilities for where we might go next, and how we could each take part.

Saving Portland Works
Derek Morton, Chair of 'Save Portland Works' 2009-11 then of Portland Works LS Ltd 2011-13

Early Days, the Campaign

My first visit to Portland Works was in 2009, on a dark, drizzly November afternoon. Scruffy, neglected and unloved, not promising. Yet the magic so many people have felt about this place took hold of me. 130 years of continuous making by countless Sheffielders along with half a century of extreme neglect had created a scene not often found in the City.

An example of neglect – a blocked modified doorway, peeling paint, damp plasterboard ...

Looking at the building ten years later it is hard to imagine the state it was in at that time. Dumped rubbish and abandoned machinery everywhere. Buddleia growing from gutters and high brickwork. Pigeons everywhere. Damaged roofs, leaking gutters and broken, patched and paintless windows. So many windows! Even so it was clear that under the neglect there was a fine building, well designed and purposeful, from the street-side archway and curved sash windows with fine brick detailing, to the modular look of the internal ranges with matching casement windows and nice touches like the brick arches and rounded bull-nose bricks on window and door surrounds.

At this point, Portland Works had been owned for forty years by a succession of property speculators, waiting for the optimum moment for redevelopment. Longer-standing tenants despaired at the continuing decline. Rents were low, true, but expectations were low as well. Most workshops were damp, draughty and unheated. The electricity network was distinctly dangerous, with decades-old cotton and perished rubber covered cables in the shambolic meter-rooms. Quite a few units were simply used for storage, and at least one large unit had been the scene of many rave parties. Yet the 'live' tenants had made conditions within their accommodation to make the units comfortable in their own way, often with a home-made stove.

On that November afternoon, it was the Galvanise Festival, aimed at showing off the City's metalworking heritage, and here were two fine metalworkers in Stuart Mitchell and Andy Cole. Within the neglect their workshops were havens of warmth and activity on that winter's day, and the small group of visitors were entranced as Andy forged white hot steel into chisels and Stuart ground and polished his elegant knives.

I was impressed with Stuart and Andy's approach to their work, valuing traditional hand craft work blended with a few modern techniques. Stuart had taken on his father's struggling cutlery business and transformed it, making high quality bespoke knives for customers over the world. I was also impressed to see a Victorian forge workshop, almost unchanged, still in regular use by Andy to make builder's tools. It turned out there were other tenants with a long history of metalworking and engineering in Portland Works (Mick Shaw, Pam Hague, Jimmy Holmes, Richard Whiteley to name a few) alongside woodworkers (Paul Hopprich, Kevin Burgin and Lynthorpe), several artists led by Alison Douglas and Claire Hughes, and musicians, including 'The Gentlemen' carrying on Def Leppard's legacy here, and newer ones putting a new spin on old techniques - such as Pete Ledger and Mark Jackson.

It was astonishing to discover that Andy's forge was the very same place Harry Brearley had worked with Ernest Stuart in 1914 to make his first stainless steel knives. Apart from the electric motors and strip lights, much was original and well over a century old. Not only that, but manufacturing had never stopped at Portland Works. Mosley's business had ended in the 1960s, but other cutlery and related makers had been tenants long before then, and continued to the present day.

I was appalled to discover the place was threatened with a planning application for conversion into flats, just resubmitted a week or so earlier. This would inevitably result in the eviction of all the tenants, destruction of the forge and other workshops, and conversion into 85 'studio flats'. This was at a time when blocks of flats seemed to be springing up everywhere around the ring road and the market looked saturated, with people pleading for houses!

The following week I wrote to the Sheffield Telegraph and started getting phone calls. Following this I joined the campaigners - Julia Udall (Community Architectural Researcher at Sharrow Community Forum), local Councillor Jillian Creasy, Alan Deadman of Stag Works and about a dozen of the tenants at Cafe Euro (now Harland Cafe in John St), just before Christmas. It was quite an experience - everyone loved the Works, but it quickly became clear that there would be precious few legal grounds for opposing the application, given the Works' dilapidated state as an industrial building, and the inevitable prospect seemed to be the conversion of the Works into flats.

Our group, on the other hand, had all grasped that what the Works had was 'living heritage', something very special for Sheffield. Yet, rather than valuing and celebrating what Portland Works had, we could all be looking at its destruction. The last Sheffield cutlery works building to be in continuous use for manufacturing faced conversion into flats.

There was an air of despondency. If the planning application was turned down, the landlord would probably seek to raise rents and, on the evidence of the past, offer very little in return. Then put in another application. And how could we get out of the game of just opposing the flats? What would become of the Works? It was clear that the building needed a lot of work, needing far more cash than the rents might ever generate, so how might that be financed? Even so, someone voiced what could have been in everyone's thoughts - 'Why not buy it?'

The Steering Group

By 12 January 2010 Julia had organised a public meeting at Sharrow Community Forum - 'Portland Works Alternative Futures'. At the previous meeting we'd already raised the possibility of buying out the Works to secure its future, and a plan was growing. We looked at a vision for the future, potential management and building priorities. We saw the Works as a place of creativity, traditional crafts and small scale manufacturing. New businesses could be encouraged, the old skills passed on. We would work this up to a business plan which would inform all our press, media and political work over the next few months.

A Steering Group became the main focus for action, meeting every two weeks. A core group of about 20 people - tenants and members of the community - led the campaign in a cooperative spirit. Meetings were circular, everyone an equal partner plus a Chair for the rare occasions when order was needed. I found myself co-opted as Chair, a position I held with pride for the next three years. The focus and work output was extraordinary. Cooperation and consensus powered by enthusiasm and a sense of destiny can achieve a lot. It was great fun too, carrying on into the post-meeting socials at the Cremorne or a local curry house.

We undertook an audit of the Works to see who exactly was working there. It transpired that 35 people were actively using the Works, via 20 tenants. They covered a wide range of metal and woodworking trades and creative industries. Almost every unit in the Works was occupied. In fact, far from being under-used and under-occupied as claimed in the planning application, the Works was clearly contributing positively to the local economy.

What followed was a long and grinding process to get attention through press and media. The focus had shifted from defeating the planning application to buying the Works. After that the planning issue became less important as delays added up and discussions around buying the Works took off. We needed a lot of professional advice too, and it came.

Alan Deadman of Stag Works offered a huge amount of support from an early stage and offered the good offices of the Little Sheffield Development Trust, itself formed (unsuccessfully) to buy out Stag Works some years earlier. Their experience in attempting a buy-out steeled us for a long haul. But they put us on to the Cooperative Society and their support for small co-op start-ups. Like us.

Julia knew about the Architectural Heritage Fund (AHF) whose normal business is supporting Building Preservation Trusts to rescue derelict listed buildings. Their advice in these early stages was hugely appreciated, and it was wonderful to meet a group of people who knew about old buildings and could see exactly what we were about. They also eventually became our main lender.

We set up a website to complement the existing blog and Facebook page, as a 'one stop' place which kept the public up to date and allowed them to contact us. Messages came in from all over the world. Meanwhile the arts scene was buzzing around the Works - a major photography exhibition in Castle Market through February to April featured the Works and produced a wonderful petition of support, and Bank Street Arts offered space to the Portland artists to promote the cause. Offers of help resulted in a set of vibrant posters of Portland works tenants, which we pasted onto the street side of the Works. The Sheffield Photographers group used us as a basis for more than one exhibition and got our message out to a whole new section of Sheffield.

BBC Calendar, Yorkshire Post, Radio Sheffield and the Sheffield Telegraph and Star all ran pieces on the Works. Radio 4 'You and Yours' ran a ten minute piece in May 2011 and we made Sky News. Several tenants became media stars and we'd reached national coverage! The Council came 'onside' following a visit by the Council leader Paul Scriven who recognised the Works' contribution to Sheffield's history and economy.

Re-Imagining Portland Works

Julia's contacts and hard work with the University led to a £10,000 grant from the University under its Knowledge Transfer Partnership, to fund an important conference / workshop in June 2010. This brought in a lot of experts and ourselves to consider how the Portland Works campaign group's future priorities would translate into buying, owning and managing. The workshop drew in expertise from throughout the region and made stakeholders aware of what was important about Portland Works. The outcome of the day was a decision to form an Industrial Provident Society (now known as a Community Benefit Society) as the preferred model of purchase. The steering group became the Portland Works Committee and support came from the Cooperative Enterprise Hub to write a formal business plan.

We registered our Community Benefit Society. It's a limited company owned by its members, but the benefits go to the wider community as well as the members who have invested.

Hundreds of people had opposed the flats. Without our protest, the flats would have happened. Here was a real opportunity to get something right, to demonstrate what a community could achieve.

During the summer 2010 Stuart and I met the owner and in several rather tense meetings, we secured an offer in principle to sell the Works to our group, without a price being agreed. It was clear that we'd reached a turning point. But first he (the owner) wanted to 'see the money'. This was getting serious.

Raising cash

We started holding open days. Initially rather hit and miss, we managed to bring in 100-200 people each time, many of whom donated cash for the campaign and were enlisted into the growing group of potential supporters.

Early 2011 seemed a blur of activity. A team of five wrote a business plan, subjected to endless edits and rewriting, and in frenzies of activity bashed it into a coherent shape which could be presented to the world. Our work achieved credibility. In June 2011 I was contacted by Hugh Facey OBE who said 'I've read your business plan...' (few people actually do this!) '... and I like it!' We negotiated loans from two sources, AHF and the equally helpful Key Fund South Yorkshire. We were ticking their boxes.

The share launch was on 16 June 2011. A party of several hundred supporters turned up at the Works, the wine flowed, the band played, it was a proper sunny evening and we took our first £7,500 of share sales. Press interest was intense and it seemed we were in our way. Money continued to flow in and by September we were at £100,000 and the owners started to notice. We knew we had to make £200,000 to have a hope of negotiating a deal. The money went into a holding account quite separate from our rapidly vanishing campaign account. We thought we'd be there in six months ... and we had to be able to return the cash if we failed. We now had several hundred shareholders who were trusting us with their cash, but also very willing to help in all sorts of ways.

Hugh Facey facilitated the negotiations and provided sage advice. As the discussions got under way through the late autumn we struggled to get further with the fundraising, and by January 2012 we were on £115,000, not wonderful. The share offer was due to close in January - so we extended it.

Two things then happened. The previous September a film crew had come from the BBC to make 'Heritage Heroes' with John Craven. We'd forgotten about it but it went out in early February on mainstream television, coincidentally in the same week that we launched a press and media blitz. Our share sales took off again, as people all over the country put in cash - we took over £30,000 from 70 new contacts in six weeks as well as taking £2,000 of donations. An open day on a sunny day in March lifted our spirits, it seemed we might be on the way after all.

The second thing was to make a deal with the owners. In April 2012, almost at the point of pulling out when it felt we may not reach the common ground, we agreed a price and a process to get there, thanks very much to Hugh Facey's efforts. This deal - which in the end failed - involved a staged purchase over three years that we could finance with our resources, whilst providing a fair price for the owners. It was generally agreed to be fair to both parties. But it was to be another twelve months before we got there. We continued, slowly, to sell shares but seemed to stick well short of £200,000. We had a £100,000 loan from AHF, and meanwhile the legal difficulties with the contract just grew, along with the bill.

Finally, in January 2013 we cleared the logjam. AHF doubled their loan offer to £200,000 which meant we only (only!) had to raise another £100,000 to clear a new purchase price, pay the legal fees and have a bit to spare to start the building work. Hugh reckoned we could do that - 'ask the shareholders' - and he was right. The gamble paid off and shareholders came up with another £40,000 of shares sales. We bridged the gap with a Bond offer - which raised another £60,000. A 'final' cash offer was made and accepted, and with great speed, the deal was 'done' on the last day of February 2013. The Works became entirely ours.

Owners!

Buying the Works was a long and tortuous business, and it certainly took its toll in the stress levels of several key members, including myself, but the group moved on to the job of running the Works. Despite months of preparation it was hard! Colin Havard was employed as manager -

initially for a day a week but soon hiked up to 3.5, and well worth it. He managed the project in the Works for three years and we will always be grateful for his guidance and ability to get along with all parties. I relinquished the Chair late in 2013 and handed over to Nikky Wilson.

We achieved national recognition as 'Heritage Heroes' at an award ceremony by the Heritage Alliance, in December 2013 at the Royal Geographical Society London, I was proud to make a presentation about the campaign along with Nikky, plus Stuart Mitchell - later to become Chair - and Julia Udall. At that time we'd only just gained ownership, and looking back it's fair to say that was only half the battle.

Friends of Portland Works was set up as an independent fund-raising charitable arm to support renovation and education work. It has steadily explored many new avenues of funding and brought in significant sums to help our work. Along with an HLF grant in 2016 for both roof-work and an education and outreach worker, we have managed to stay ahead in the financial game.

A year later and we were able to say the roof was weatherproofed (only just - it didn't last long!) and we'd stopped the entrance portico on its slow journey to street level through stabilisation and renovation. Two cracked and crumbling ground floor pillars in 'C block' were very expensively restored with additional steel reinforcement and a lot of calculations.

New switchgear appeared in the main meter rooms to protect our tenants (and the building) along with a decent fire alarm system. We began our first 'proper renovation' of the old 'showroom' area of the Works. What was the site of many rave parties in the last decade was cleared by volunteers - six skips - restored and transformed into three workshops and a large studio. Crucially, it was now earning us money as we'd spent most of our reserve.

Subsequent years saw the growth from a tiny group of volunteers - Bill Gray, Chris Cooper and half a dozen others at the start - to a regular gang of 15 or so helpers, multi skilled and enthusiastic, who work most Tuesdays and in late 2018 passed the halfway stage for restored windows together with new pointing and restored masonry. Whole sections of the Works have now been renovated. Much remains of course at the time of writing, but the efforts of Friends of Portland Works plus the continuing kindness of individual donors has kept the volunteers in paint, putty, mortar and tools. There are over 250 windows at Portland Works, and it is a tribute to Victorian buildings that the majority of these rotten-looking pitch pine windows can be rescued, in-filled and reglazed. Inside we have restored around 15 workshops - this includes new wiring and lighting - and supported several tenants in enhancing their own spaces. In 2016-17 we created a small museum area and a large public space for meetings and education work.

Despite two blocks still almost untouched, there's a sense that the Works is looking the way it should - a cared-for working environment. Tenants value the sense of community and the unique ambience that is Portland Works. It's certainly not over-restored - possibly more the other way - but we have become the place where the Sheffield's past meets its future.

There's still a mountain to climb, but we will make it.

These pictures show a 'case study' of renovation in progress. This is one of the original hand-forges, still with a split 'stable-door' but with a glazed window instead of an iron grid. It has been completely renovated in an original style, and a new brick floor was laid with damp-proofing. The unit is now finished, and let to Locksley's, who have fitted it out for gin-tastings.

Tenants of today

In a very real sense Portland Works is the home of stainless steel manufacturing and that is its historic importance. But now, having been saved as a working environment, it has a future as a place of 'making' and is still important today. As improvements have been made, more space is being provided for a variety of craftspeople and artists. The surroundings are such that noise is not generally an issue for neighbours; the nearest are across quite a busy road.

Some of the tenants would have felt at home in the metal-works of a century ago: knife-maker, engraver, silver-plater, tool maker and so on. There are also joiners with workshops, artists and sculptors with studios, and music groups using the buildings as rehearsal space. This chapter tells you, briefly, about some of them. You can contact any of them through links on the Portland Works website.

We begin with a few tenants who have been at Portland Works for over 30 years – in some cases for all their working lives. Andrew Cole and Stuart Mitchell were both part of the group which fought to prevent the development of the building into student accommodation.

Stuart Mitchell Knives

Stuart Mitchell and Portland Works share a long history. Stuart first arrived as a small boy around 1980 with his parents (who had previously been based at Stag Works) and their hopes of growing a knife making business. He completed a traditional knife-makers apprenticeship with his dad and eventually went on to take over the business. Over three decades later he still makes knives in the same workshop at Portland Works.

Although he still uses many of the original tools and works in the very same space, both the making process and the quality of the finished product have diversified and improved significantly in order to compete in the modern day world marketplace. Understanding the need to embrace change and new ways of working has ensured that his business is still trusted and flourishing to this day.

Stuart's custom-built knives attract a lot of attention, and today his knives are used in many contexts across the world.

'My trade, in my lifetime, I've seen that dwindle away. There are definitely skills and traditions that are still worth keeping alive. I can't think of many people after me that will be able to do it.'

He remembers vividly coming to Portland Works for the first time. 'I was at school on Solly Street and I remember my Dad picking me up from school to bring me to the new premises, it was like a momentous family occasion. Before I had been to Stag and pottered around, but here I felt more part of the business because I'd been part of moving, like a fresh start.'

When his parents moved in, empty bits of the Works were dirty, quite an adventure, and 'a bit spooky' as well. The whole front block first floor was empty and still set up as old offices, with all the fireplaces in place. It has only been more fully occupied in the last 20 years or so; this is probably because other similar places have been closing. Now, because of its heritage, people actually want to be here.

Andrew Cole Tools

Andy has worked at Portland Works since 1978 – over forty years. He began with Wigfull Tools, working for Eric Wigfull, but more recently has set up his own company forging made-to-measure tools. Wigfull Tools was always in the forge, and Andy still is, working some of the original equipment installed by Mosley's.

As time has gone on, imports from China have been imported more cheaply than steel could be bought in this country and Andy has had to change the focus of what he does.

Andy's hand-crafted tools are now made to measure and are sent all over the world: there is still a demand for handmade wood chisels, and

Andy's have a lifetime guarantee. He also works with those who want to keep hand-forging skills alive, allowing access to his premises.

PH Engineering

Pam Hague is 70 and is still in her workshop most days. Her speciality is lino-cutting tools and she makes around 2,000 a month. An example is to the right. She starts with a 6-foot rod of steel and cuts it into two and three-quarter inch lengths. Then with a double-headed drill she drills each end, to leave a fine blade - after which the steel must be tempered.

After tempering she grinds it to a 5-degree angle. It is all very small and intricate work, which is easier for a woman with her smaller hands.

Pam's father was Ray Wildsmith, who had worked with Harry Brearley and for Joseph Rodgers. He left Rodgers about 1964 and became self-employed in Shoreham Street, and used to sharpen knives for the meat market – all knives were sharpened most weeks.

In about 1968 Ray moved to Portland Works. Pam was working for Marks & Spencer at the time, but did all Ray's accounts for him. Ray worked at various things, including making pen-knives and the like. He also helped Emil Berek and his wife to make jewellery. They were very busy making rings, chains and all kinds of jewellery, and relatives used to come to the Works to help Ray – including his wife and two sisters. Berek's office was in the nearby workshop on the street range. A former window high up in Pam's workshop enabled Emil to 'spy' on the staff from his office, even though there is no direct connection. But all that came to an end when Berek and his wife were killed in a car crash.

After that Wildsmith started welding for a firm in Chesterfield who made parts for central heating. It was a booming trade in those days. Ray died at the age of 85, but was still working. 'This yard was amazing. They were all doing metalwork and everyone did everything. You could ask anyone for help and they would give it to you.' A big task he took on was making metal gridded fencing for the National Trust at Stoke – an intricate job. Every piece had to fit to the ground, even though the levels were uneven. To make the fence the steel lengths were formed, galvanised, and wound around with thin wire. Some pieces were ten feet high so it needed bigger equipment than he had, and Arthur Lay in the yard made Wildsmith's a welder. The whole job took four years, but it took Wildsmith a long time to receive payment for what he had done.

Shaw Engraving

Shaw Engraving is a well established Sheffield company serving a wide range of UK industries with specialised handstamps and machine dies, engraved sign work, and specialist marking services. Mick Shaw, the owner, has been at Portland Works for around 40 years.

Mick has an array of engraving machines in his tiny workshop, producing extremely high quality results with scaling, milling and machining equipment.

He makes stamps, punches and bespoke engraving jobs for customers all over the world. He also enjoys working at Portland Works because of the friendliness and the co-operation of other tenants in borrowing machines and so on.

Other tenants have been at the Works for varying amounts of time – there are no implications in the order they appear in!

Tietzsch Guitars

Thom Tietzsch Tyler makes rather beautiful electric guitars. He started around 2015, working in a small shop for a couple of years learning his craft before taking on his present larger unit which incorporates his own paint spray facility. He uses fine and unusual woods, choosing carefully and working with skill and patience, striving to give his beautiful guitars a 'bit of magic'. Thom believes a good guitar combines aesthetics with good materials and high levels of skill. His hero is Semie Moseley (!) of California who made much sought after guitars around 60 years ago.

Bailey of Sheffield

Bailey of Sheffield creates stainless steel jewellery engineered to last a lifetime. That doesn't just mean durable high calibre materials or timeless design; it's about understated pieces that adapt with you and your changing style. Each piece is all about you – a place to curate your own personal style – we just give you a firm, well forged foundation.

Crafted from the highest quality marine grade 316L stainless steel, both the CABLE stainless steel bracelet and stainless steel necklace range are hand built in our workshop in Sheffield situated at Portland Works, the birthplace of stainless steel manufacturing.

Ben Daniels

Ben started at Portland Works from nothing, originally with his brother. He now creates beautiful hand-made toys and unique items in his first-floor workshop. He only uses second-hand and reclaimed timber from around Sheffield.

Sheffield Hackspace *Sheffield Hardware Hackers and Makers CIC*

This is a non-profit, member-run hackspace for the city of Sheffield and the surrounding areas. Over the last couple of years we have created communal workshops and a community who share skills and help each other with projects and ideas including, but not limited to: electronics (including Arduino, Raspberry Pi, and ESP8266), LoRAWAN, 3D printing and CAD, textiles (including wearable electronics), robotics, woodwork and metalwork, arts and crafts, gaming, photography and use of the Internet of Things (IoT).

Ultimately, we are member led. Some of the projects get highlighted on our website (https://www.sheffieldhackspace.org.uk), but there's no substitute for coming along to meet the group. We're always keen for people with a wide range of interests and skill levels to join, swap ideas, learn from each other, and build new things.

If you're interested, drop us an email (see the website for details) or come along to one of our open sessions to see what we're about.

Michael May Knives

Michael May worked for Taylor Eyewitness for 14 years before striking out on his own in a tiny workshop here. Around that time he acquired famous local knife maker Trevor Ablett's tools and stock, a great start.

He soon grew out of the first shop and now has a larger ground floor unit where he makes up to 20 knives a week. Mainly traditional folding pocket knives, they are very often in unusual materials like damascus steel, hand forged elsewhere in the Works. Handles in Yorkshire oak are a favourite too. Recently he's been joined by James Rhodes, who is rapidly learning the trade.

Portland Works Studio

Portland Works Studio is the studio base of commercial photographer Carl Whitham. Carl originally trained as a forensic photographer, then moved on to work for the Royal Photographic Society in Bath where he also set up his own studio in 1996. He has built up a reputation as a highly adaptable studio and location photographer producing dynamic imagery for commercial, advertising and editorial purposes.

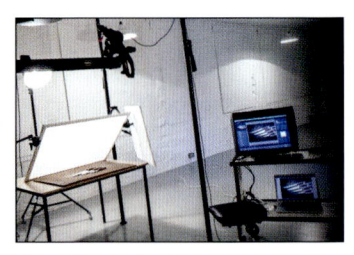

Much of the work focuses on the industrial sector where Carl's experience and technical ability allows him to produce creative, inspiring images in very challenging environments ranging from Sheffield steel foundries to UK-wide manufacturing and European technical centres.

Since a lot of Carl's work takes place on location, his studio is often available for hire, providing a unique and flexible workspace for photography and photographic workshops.

The studio space has been sympathetically refurbished to show the original Victorian architecture with north & south-facing windows providing amazing amounts of natural light when required. It is equipped with blackout blinds, loading bay, fully fitted kitchen, dressing room and a huge quantity of modern photographic studio equipment.

PML Plating

PML Plating Ltd was formed in 2009 by Peter Ledger, a silver plater who began working in the industry in 1978. Sadly, Peter found himself redundant after the firm he worked for within the city went into administration.

Peter, having excellent knowledge of the industry, saw that silver plating was still an industry that could thrive and decided to use his savings to start his own plating company. He is now probably one of the only independent silver platers in the city.

The company has two managing directors - husband and wife team Peter & Sue Ledger - and some excellent staff including Claire our warehouse manager who again has many years of experience in warehousing and Emma (Peter's daughter) who is here to complete the lacquering of the knife blades and administration tasks for the company and to look into ways we can continue to thrive for many years to come.

The Ledger family are very proud of their heritage, coming from a family who have worked in the key industries that form part of the steel city's legacy. Peter's father worked in the steel works and Sue's mother worked in many elements of the cutlery industry including being a buffer girl. They use this enthusiasm for Sheffield and its history to bring this to life in every element of their work and pride themselves on providing an excellent service and end product, using traditional methods.

PML Plating Ltd celebrated their 10th anniversary in 2019.

Locksley Distilling

Locksley Distilling Co. Ltd. is an active distillery, and alcoholic beverage development company, founded by Sheffield born John Cherry when he relocated from New York with his family in 2013. Having worked in the wine and spirits industry for the preceding two decades, it was his wife (who's a New Yorker) who persuaded him to return home to pursue his dream of setting up an English distillery.

After John had tested 104 recipes in development, Locksley launched their first gin, Sir Robin of Locksley®, in the summer of 2014, doffing the cap to local Sheffield-born legend Robin Hood.

This coincided with the early days of what was to become an explosion in the popularity of gin in the U.K., which enabled the company to take residence in Portland Works. From 2015 every drop has been distilled, bottled, and labelled on site.

In 2018 Locksley took on the original steam engine room as their bottling unit, to alleviate the logistical issues of running thousands of glass bottles up and down from their first floor distillery. And in 2019 they extended into a third space within Portland Works.

Keen to share their passion, share their story, and offer total transparency of their process, the third space (the best-preserved example of a working forge on site) serves as a 'gin school' to offer visitors the chance to create and develop their own unique gins.

Buffer Girl Jewellery

Emma's father is Peter, a silver plater in the city of Sheffield (above!), who has worked in the industry for over 30 years. Over his many years in the industry he has been offered lots of scrap cutlery. It was after seeing a similar idea that I decided to ask him to make a bracelet using some of the scrap cutlery for my sister-in-law, who is Russian and who adores anything Sheffield and appreciates the quality and significance of Sheffield cutlery.

It was after having many admirers of the bracelet that we decided to 'upcycle' some of the many items we have and make them into beautiful pieces of jewellery.

Our items are hand-made here in the Portland Works from old EPNS blanks we have hanging around our silver plating shop, that have been collected over the years.

We do where possible try to use Sheffield blanks - however we have a collection of blanks that were originally made in France too and other odds and ends.

The Portland Works artists

Mary Sewell is a practising artist who moved into Portland Works in 2007. She has been a tenant for the past 13 years. In 2016 she moved from where Locksley Gin's office is now based to the Lantern Room. It is a wonderful space for a visual artist with the light from the roof and it is here that she paints and sculpts using clay, pigment and found objects sourced from Sheffield's industrial quarters. She also painted the evocative Portland Ghost after being told the story by Andy Cole who saw the ghost one night while working at Wigfull Tools.

Leslie Wilson has had a space at Portland Works since 2011, after being invited to join by Clare Hughes - one of the founders of the studio. At that time the buildings and yards were a rich source of material for a visual artist: rusting steel plates were one example of found objects from which many images were created. The studio provided Leslie with the space to play and work experimentally on a large scale with various processes: printing, dyeing, papermaking and collage. The environment and people of the Works continue to provide inspiration while her subject matter has inevitably changed over time.

Linda Doughty had been friends of the other artists for several years, and moved into the studio next to the Lantern Room in September 2017. Before then she worked from home. Being in the studio has given her the opportunity to explore more techniques and increase the size of her canvases. Working with mixed media, Linda is inspired by nature and by Portland Works itself: the views from her windows have led her to appreciate the architecture and sounds of daily life around her, and led to the use of lines and shapes within her paintings.

A new Blacksmith!

Pete and James are (at the time of writing) moving into a workshop at Portland Works and will be working as blacksmiths. They are equipping a forge, and their work will be done by hand.

Squarepegs

Mark Jackson's Squarepegs takes raw materials to produce his unusual patented coat hook system for schools, using a mix of traditional and high technology processes. A start-up business in 2006, Squarepegs installations are being put in all over the country.

The Squarepegs system was designed to prevent coats falling to the floor, whilst keeping children safe from collision with exposed hooks. The unique patented design configures the pegs so that, rather than serving to dislodge each other, even the bulkiest coats help one another to stay where they're put. The safety rail running in front of the pegs prevents collision between heads and pegs, and for added safety the rounded corners are fitted with rubber buffers.

The Squarepegs workshop is housed in the part of the Works originally occupied by grinding wheels in Mosley's day, and features a brick-vaulted ceiling.

Lynthorpe Woodworks

At Lynthorpe Woodworks we have over 25 years of experience in the manufacture and installation of hardwood and softwood windows, doors, staircases and conservatories. As a family run business, we promise to provide you with a personal service which will exceed your expectations. A majority of our work comes from repeat business and recommendations proving our fantastic service.

Based in Sheffield, we offer our services in the surrounding areas including Chesterfield, Rotherham, Doncaster and Barnsley. Work is also carried out in London and surrounding areas.

Opus Independents

Opus believes we can live in a place where everyone works to make things better for each other. 'Better' to us means fair, diverse, accessible, independent and heard. That's why we champion social causes, independent business, not-for-profits, emerging talent and healthy debate from our base at Portland Works.

Since 2008, we've run projects like Now Then Magazine, Wordlife and Festival of Debate – they connect us to each other and to music, arts, culture, ideas, action and conversations that will make change.

And more than anything, that's what we're here for: to make it easier to contribute to change for the better – and to have fun doing it.

Pippa Elliott

Pippa Elliott is one of the few hand-tufting rug makers in the country – making both her own designs and commissions here in Sheffield.

Coming from a wool producing family, her passion for rugs came from her travels and living overseas in the Middle East. She is currently working on a series of rugs that combine old repaired Persian rugs with new bright vibrant yarn sourced from Yorkshire mills.

Wilebore Leather

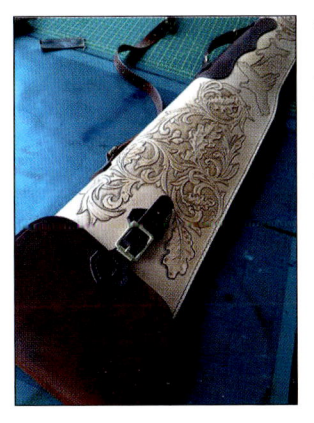

Wilebore Leather has been at Portland Works since February 2019, run by its founder Kevin Wilebore. He began making seats for Lambrettas at home, and was soon asked by friends to make other things in leather, which he is increasingly doing. He uses traditional tools and methods, all of it by hand.

Kevin has a commission with Ernest Wright Scissormakers of Sheffield, for whom he makes scissor-holsters; as well as bringing sales, this gives him excellent exposure.

Lowtech Ltd

Lowtech is all about exploring the potential of emerging technologies, and has a history of research into the impacts of digital manufacture on local jobs and enterprises. We use laser cutters to produce "Infinite Crypt", modular architecture for tabletop miniatures gaming. The popularity of games like "Dungeons & Dragons" makes this a very exciting niche market, with huge growth potential.

But the beauty of digital manufacture is that you can reprogram machine tools to produce just about anything! So we're open to commissions and projects which make use of our laser cutters. We can use them to produce models, signage, stencils, jewellery, prototypes and much more, using a wide range of acrylics, plastics and wood products. We're also keen to link up with researchers that are looking into the potentials of high-tech making.

Quality Cabinetry

Paul Hopprich has been making fine woodwork, fitted kitchens and bespoke furniture for about 30 years. He works with real wood and traditional materials. He makes all the organic cabinets, paints them and has a team to fit them.

'It's a beautiful building when you see beyond the dereliction. But the more important thing to me is the community spirit,' he says. All the different craftsmen at the Works help each other out, so most jobs do not have to be outsourced.

Andy Cole working on an original grinding-wheel in his workshop
Photograph taken by Will Roberts, May 2013

Looking to the future

Portland Works is now the only remaining integrated cutlery factory in Sheffield that is still in use by makers. Moreover, some of those makers are still blacksmiths and cutlery makers. The other works have all been demolished or converted. I hope Robert Mosley would be pleased with the creative and innovative use being made of his premises.

Since it was bought by over 500 people, only six or seven years ago, the amount of work that has been done to preserve the building has been astounding. The majority of this work has been done by volunteers, with the mostly enthusiastic co-operation of the tenants. They have prevented more than one part of the building from imminent (and probably final) collapse. They have worked around the building at the same time as the roofs were being replaced, to economise on scaffolding costs, and repaired the walls and windows. Most roofs are now watertight, and insulated, which is a huge improvement.

Portland Works is still a working environment, but there are several times each year that you can come to an event or on an open day to see it, or be taken on a tour. Just see our website for details.

Every time we use a steel blade, and are able simply to wash it after use, we owe a debt of gratitude to this historic place and to its visionary first owner.

Footnotes

[1] This account has to lean heavily on cuttings and newspaper articles. I have not been able to trace all of them.
[2] *Sheffield Daily Independent,* Saturday 2 February 1924 p7 and 11
[3] *Northern Star,* Lismore, 19 Dec 1916
[4] Published by Longmans, reviewed *Sheffield Daily Telegraph*, Saturday 14 Nov 1903.
[5] USA Patent 1,197,256: Cutlery
[6] For the businesses of Cornelius and Richard Mosley see Jeff Warner's history of R F Mosley & Co, published electronically in late March 2013 on www.hawleytoolcollection.com/uploads/PDF/FOM%20%20A%20Short%20History%20of%20R%20F%20Mosley%20by%20Jeff%20Warner.pdf
[7] Unless another source is given, dates of 1841, 1851, 1861 etc (to 1911) refer to the national census records.
[8] *London Gazette*, 12 April 1859
[9] *Sheffield and Rotherham Independent*, Tues 7 Jan 1862
[10] House numbers throughout are quoted as in the original sources; however, renumbering took place from time to time, and the premises do not necessarily have the same number in different sources, or today.
[11] Much of the information in this paragraph comes from a variety of trade directories.
[12] *Sheffield Daily Telegraph*
[13] *London Gazette* 7 November 1873
[14] *Sheffield Daily Telegraph,* 1 May 1877
[15] *Sheffield Daily Telegraph,* 3 June 1887
[16] The National Archives photograph collection includes copies of portraits attributed on the reverse to *T.C. Turner, Photographer & Portrait Painter, 17, Upper St., Islington, and 10, Barnsbury Park, Barnsbury, N.*
[17] R Harman and J Minnis *Sheffield (*Yale U P, Pevsner Architectural Guides, 2004) p221
[18] *The Industries of Sheffield: Business Review* (c1887), quoted in Tweedale's Directory
[19] *Yorkshire Post*, 1 May 1906
[20] *Sheffield Daily Telegraph*, 23 August 1897
[21] *Jeweller & Metalworker,* 15 March 1899 p 342, quoted in John Culme, *The Directory of Gold & Silversmiths … 1838-1914,* London, 1987
[22] *Brooklyn Daily Eagle*, New York; 27 October 1907
[23] Such as the *Northern Star* of Lismore, New South Wales
[24] *Northern Star,* 19 December 1916
[25] *The Era*, 22 Oct 1887
[26] Personal communication from Geoff Tweedale
[27] *Daily Independent,* 12 April 1938
[28] Events in this paragraph are documented in *London Gazette*, 9 July 1968 and 7 December 1972

Sources and acknowledgements

My chief sources for the start of the story are all in publicly-available archives, including census returns and records of births, marriages and deaths (all familiar to those who have researched family history).

Anyone wanting to know more about the cutlery industry in Sheffield needs to be aware of two books with an immense amount of detail about the cutlers and manufacturers of Sheffield, containing far more information than I can include here. They are:

Tweedale, Geoffrey - *Tweedale's Directory of Sheffield cutlery manufacturers 1740-2013* (2nd edition by G Tweedale, distributed by lulu.com, 2013)

Tweedale, Geoffrey - *The Sheffield knife book: a history and collectors' guide* (Sheffield, Hallamshire Press, 1996).

Harry Brearley's autobiography *Knotted String* (London: Longmans Green and Co, 1941) is a very readable account of his life and the story of stainless steel.

Much is also available on the internet, but caution is needed as there is a great deal of unchecked information that is repeated until it seems to become fact. For instance, you can read in many places that Harry Brearley was buried in Sheffield Cathedral. He was not; he died in Torquay, was cremated in Devon and his ashes were scattered there.

My particular thanks as well to descendants of the Mosley and Hobson families, to Sheffield Local Studies Library and Sheffield Archives, to Geoff Tweedale for sharing a huge amount of information, to Bert Housley for working on our catalogue pictures, to Cutlers' Hall for access to their collection, to many people who remember working at Portland Works and in Randall Street, and to others who let me use their photographs. There is information from many members of the Portland Works 'family'. I have not been able to use everything, but it has all coloured what I write.

Most of all, thank you to all our tenants and volunteers.

Anna de Lange, February 2020